849 Traditional Patchwork Patterns

A Pictorial Handbook

by Susan Winter Mills

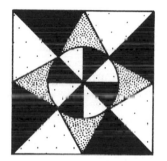

DOVER PUBLICATIONS, INC., NEW YORK

For my Allie

Published in Canada by General Publishing Company, Ltd., 30 Lesmill Road, Don Mills, Toronto, Ontario.
Published in the United Kingdom by Constable and Company, Ltd.

This Dover edition, first published in 1989, is an enlarged and corrected republication of *Illustrated Index to Traditional American Quilt Patterns,* first published by Arco Publishing, Inc., New York, in 1980 and reprinted in 1981. The "Appendix," "Index to Appendix" and "Foreword to the Enlarged Edition" have been prepared specially for the present Dover edition.

Manufactured in the United States of America
Dover Publications, Inc., 31 East 2nd Street, Mineola, N.Y. 11501

Library of Congress Cataloging-in-Publication Data

Mills, Susan Winter.
    849 traditional patchwork patterns : a pictorial handbook / by Susan Winter Mills.
        p.   cm.
    "An enlarged and corrected republication of Illustrated index to traditional American quilt patterns, first published by Arco Publishing, Inc., New York, in 1980"—T.p. verso.
    Bibliography: p.
    Includes index.
    ISBN 0-486-26003-8
    1. Quilting—United States—Patterns. 2. Patchwork—United States—Patterns. I. Mills, Susan Winter. Illustrated index to traditional American quilt patterns. II. Title.
TT835.M53   1989
746.46′041—dc19   89-30044
                                                                        CIP

Contents

Foreword to the Enlarged Edition

When this book first appeared, I was aware that there were probably many quilt patterns and names that I had not included. Since then, I have continued to research and collect patchwork patterns, and, for this new edition, I have added an Appendix containing 139 new patterns. Some of these are variations of patterns that appeared originally. In these cases, the version appearing in the original edition is considered Variation 1, even though it is not labeled as such, and the new pattern is Variation 2. (For patterns that already had several variations in the original book, the numbering continues where it left off.) A separate index for the Appendix is included.

Even now, I know that my research is far from complete. The variety of patchwork patterns and their names seems almost infinite and I am sure that there are many more blocks waiting to be discovered.

Foreword to the Original Edition

Favorite of the Peruvians, Wind Power of the Osages, Chinese 10,000 Perfections, Pure Symbol of the Right Doctrine, Battle Ax of Thor, Catch Me If You Can, Heart's Seal, Mound Builders—all names for one quilt pattern; scraps of folk poetry for the pieced-work folk art that, nurtured by necessity, flourished in pre-industrial America.

Quiltmakers were prodigiously inventive—710 quilt designs are compiled herein. They showed a remarkable sense of design and an intuitive grasp of geometrics. As many of the more popular designs spread with the settling of the nation and were repropagated in new soil, they sprang up with new names; the homogenization of language by national media was still far down the road.

My intention when I began compiling patterns was to piece together a reference tool for my own quiltmaking—something to thumb through, like a catalog, a method more conducive to inspiration than going through many books.

At first, the name for each pattern was just that—a name. After poring through the sources and finding the same pattern with different names, their profusion and poetry caught my attention. As I go through the pages now, the names delight me as much as the patterns.

Quilts warmed the Bible Belt: Tents of Armageddon, Job's Tears, Garden of Eden, Ecclesiastical.

Some names are memorials to the birth of the nation and history in the making: Burgoyne Surrounded, Underground Railroad, Sherman's March, Trail of the Covered Wagon, and Free Trade Block.

More mundane events were part of the naming. We can imagine a quiltmaker coming up with Climbing Rose after a satisfying day in the garden, or an accident in the kitchen resulting in Broken Dishes.

Individuals were honored in the naming, too: Martha Washington Star, Barbara Frietchie Star, Lincoln's Platform, and Tippecanoe and Tyler Too.

Many whimsical names were evoked by the patterns: Duck's Foot in the Mud, Pickle Dish, Drunkard's Path, and Wild Goose Chase.

Sister's Choice, Granny's Garden, Aunt Eliza's Star, Mother's Fancy Star, and Baby Bunting all reflect the importance of family; Always Friends, Nextdoor Neighbor, and Friendship Chain echo the warmth of companionship.

To put a practical face on it, collecting as many names as possible is the only sensible way to index patterns that may be known by different names in adjacent counties. In laying out the book, it was necessary to choose one "main" name for each pattern as they were arranged in sections, with secondary names for the pattern listed below the primary name. All names are included in the index to facilitate a pattern search by the reader. If the name for a quilt pattern is the object of the search, the patterns have been arranged in sections according, more or less, to the most prevalent geometric figure. (Some patterns were difficult to classify—they could easily have fallen as well into one classification as another—so I clenched my teeth and surrendered to pure arbitrariness.) After deciding what shape—triangle, square, circle, star, or combination—is predominant in your quilt, you need only thumb through that section until you recognize the pattern.

Since quilt patterns depend on the juxtaposition of light and dark fabric to bring out the design, the illustrations in this book are rendered in black and white. A quiltmaker can find a pattern he or she likes, count the shades therein, assign corresponding shades of fabric, and be assured that the quilt he makes will be a faithful rendering of the pattern.

With many patterns, using different color schemes can cause a subject-field shift or otherwise completely change the aspect of the quilt, making it hard to apprehend how it is put together. Like a blueprint, renderings of patterns in black and white bring up the details relevant to construction.

The patterns were drafted on a five-to-an-inch grid. Overlaying patterns with tracing paper with the same grid provides a unit measure for the pattern. Dividing the projected dimensions of the quilt by the number of units will indicate the size of individual blocks and pieces of the block.

Templates can then be cut to the appropriate sizes and used to trace the pieces on fabric. I cut about ¼ inch beyond and stitch on top of the traced line.

Because of their strong graphic sense, quilt patterns may be adapted for use in many areas of arts and crafts. (Z-Cross contains four figures identical to the NBC-TV logo.) Designs can also be utilized in other textile crafts such as weaving, needlepoint, and embroidery.

After I sent these patterns to the publisher, an article I wrote for my hometown paper prompted a letter from a reader with a query about and sketches of two patterns. One was among the 710 compiled here, but the other was not. I realized that the book will probably generate enough new sources and patterns to provide a diversion for many years to come.

Stars

Alice's Favorite

Arkansas Traveller
Travel Star

All Hallows

Aunt Eliza's Star

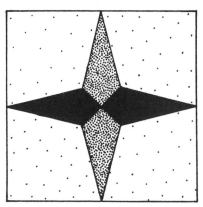

Arkansas Snowflake
Four-Point
Job's Troubles, Var. 2
Kite
Snowball, Var. 3

Beautiful Star
Arrow Star, Var. 1

Blazing Star Variation 1

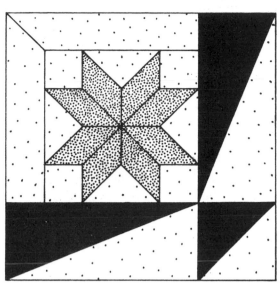

Bouquet in a Fan

Blazing Star Variation 2
Lemon Star, Var. 3

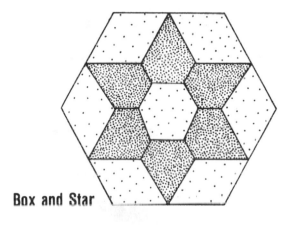

Box and Star

Blazing Sun

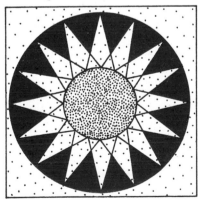

Caesar's Crown

California Star   Variation 1

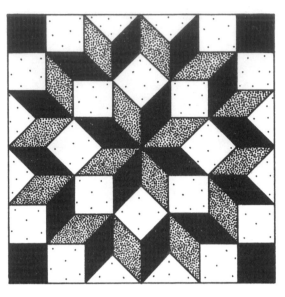

Carpenter's Wheel   Variation 2

California Star   Variation 2

Chained Star
Brunswick Star, Var. 1
Rolling Star, Var. 3

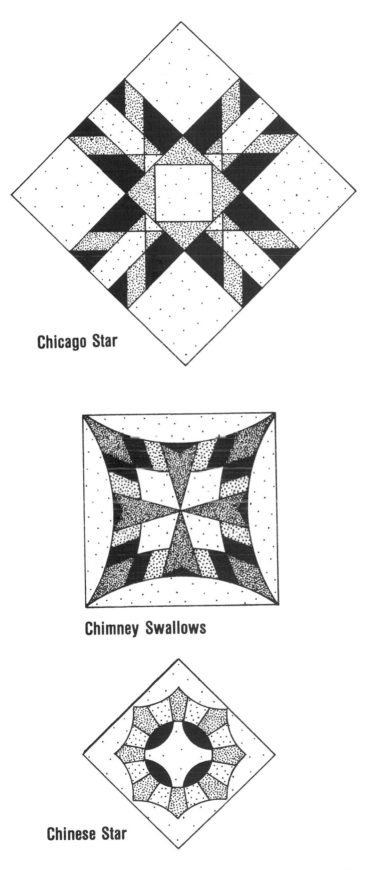

Chicago Star

Chimney Swallows

Chinese Star

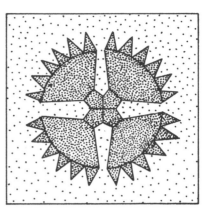

Chips and Whetstones
Variation 1

Chips and Whetstones
Variation 2

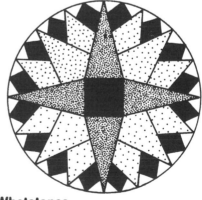

Chips and Whetstones
Variation 3

5

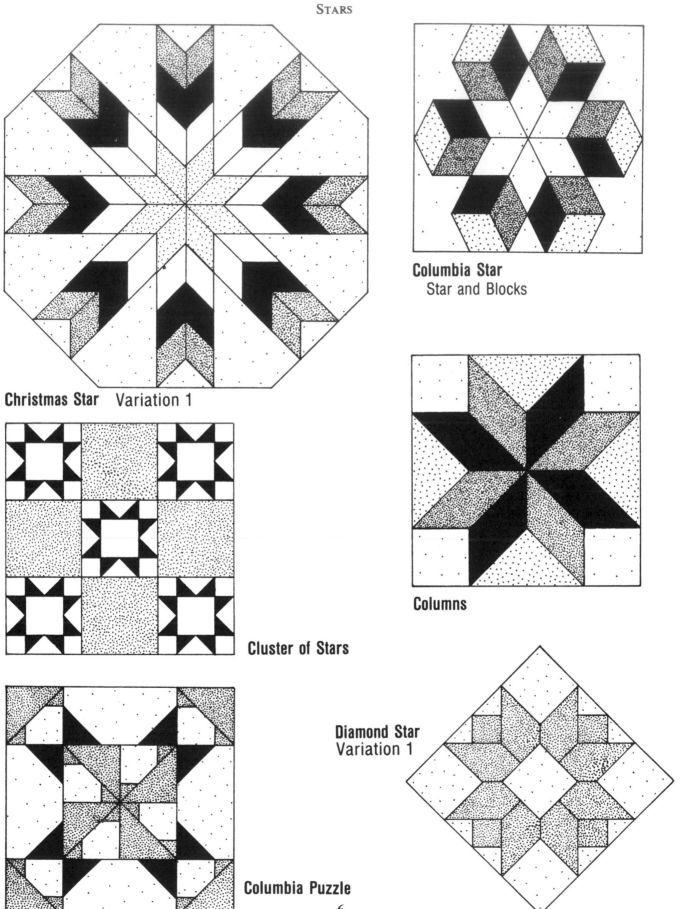

Christmas Star Variation 1

Columbia Star
Star and Blocks

Cluster of Stars

Columns

Columbia Puzzle

Diamond Star
Variation 1

6

Diamond Star   Variation 2

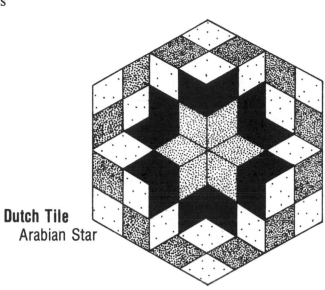

Dutch Tile
Arabian Star

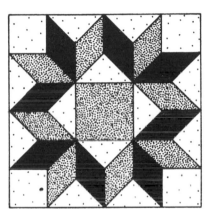

Dove at the Window

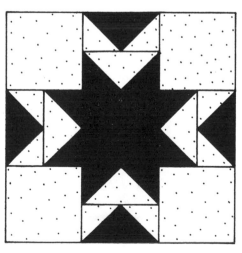

Eccentric Star   Variation 2

Dutch Rose
Octagonal Star, Var. 1

Eight-Pointed Star   Variation 2

7

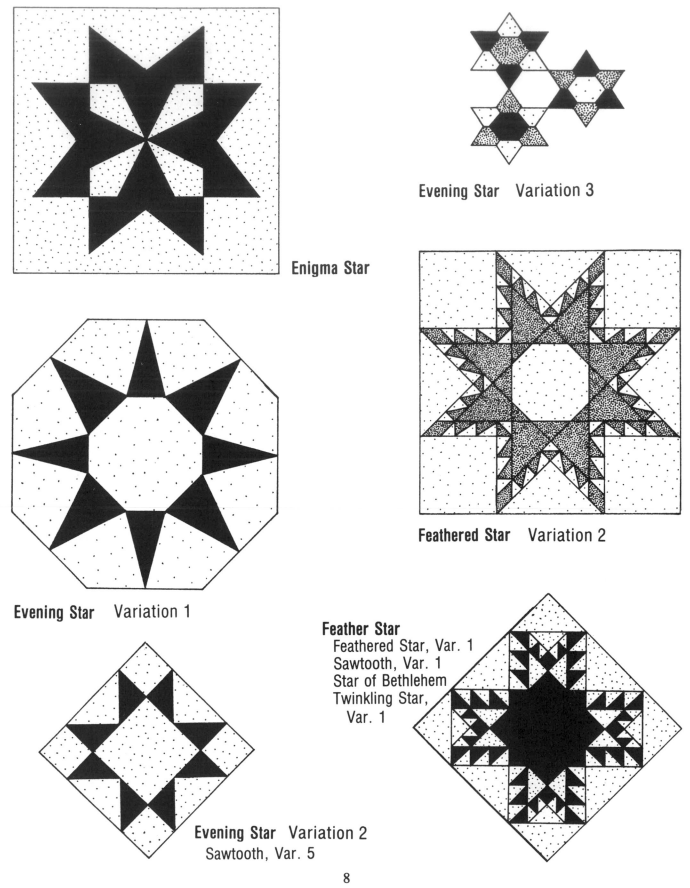

Enigma Star

Evening Star   Variation 3

Evening Star   Variation 1

Feathered Star   Variation 2

Feather Star
Feathered Star, Var. 1
Sawtooth, Var. 1
Star of Bethlehem
Twinkling Star,
    Var. 1

Evening Star   Variation 2
Sawtooth, Var. 5

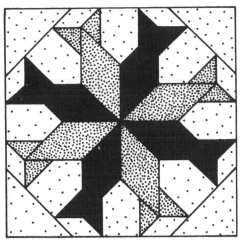

Fish Block
  Goldfish

Flying Bat
  Polaris Star

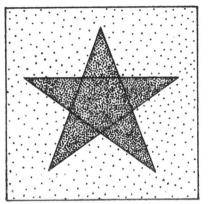

Five-Pointed Star

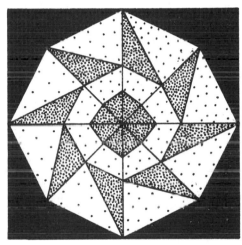

Flying Saucer

Flower Star   Variation 1

Flying Swallow
  Circling Swallows
  Falling Star
  Flying Star

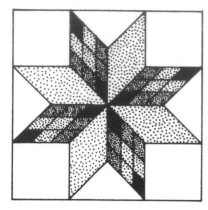

Formosa Tea Leaf

Geometric Star

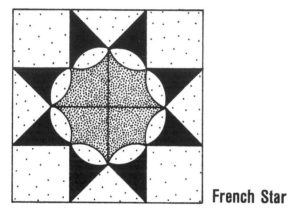

French Star

Georgetown Circle   Variation 2

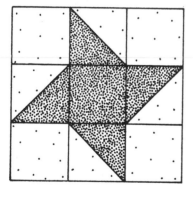

Friendship Star
Variation 1

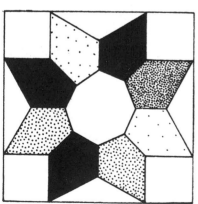

Friendship Star
Variation 2

Guiding Star

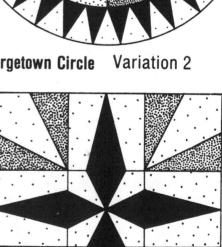

Harlequin Star

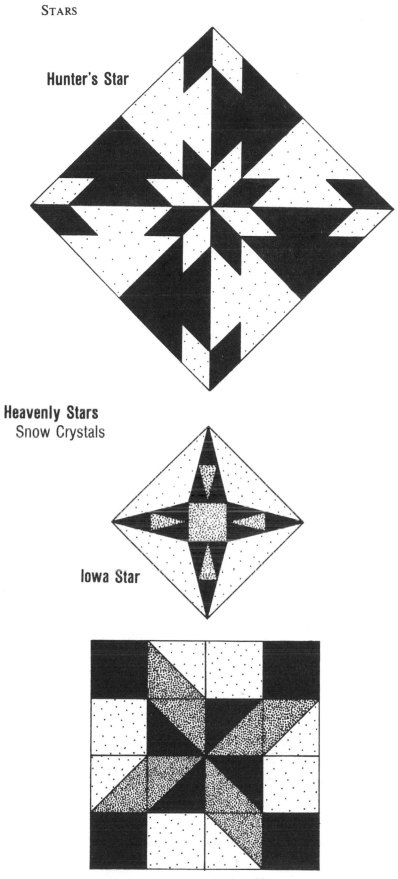

Hunter's Star

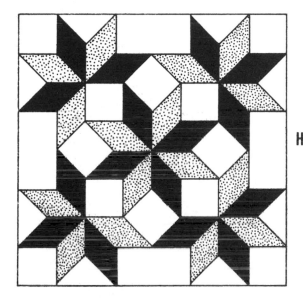

Heavenly Stars
Snow Crystals

Iowa Star

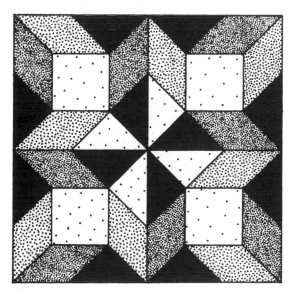

Hopscotch

Jackson's Star Variation 1

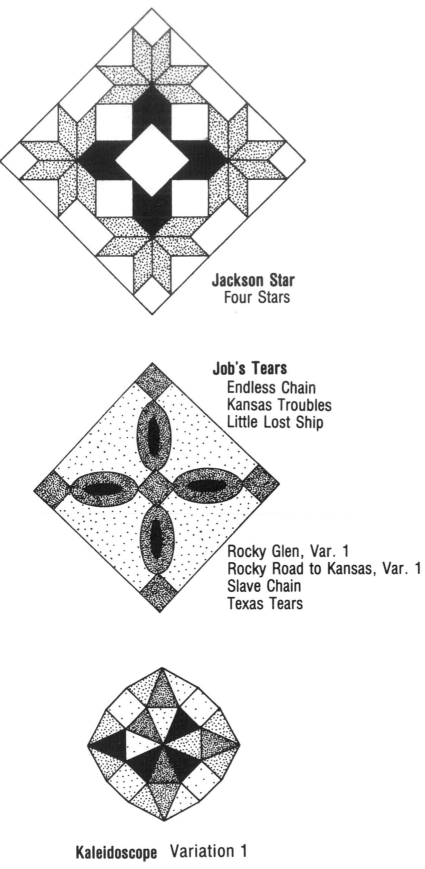

Jackson Star
Four Stars

Job's Tears
Endless Chain
Kansas Troubles
Little Lost Ship

Rocky Glen, Var. 1
Rocky Road to Kansas, Var. 1
Slave Chain
Texas Tears

Kaleidoscope Variation 1

Key West Star

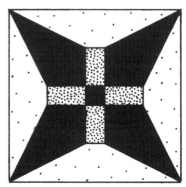

King David's Crown
Variation 1

King's Star Variation 1

Lazy Daisy Variation 2

Le Moyne Star Variation 2
Divided Star
Lemon Star, Var. 2
Star of LeMoine, Var. 2
Star of LeMoyne, Var. 2

Liberty Star

Light and Shadows

Leavenworth Star

Log Cabin Star

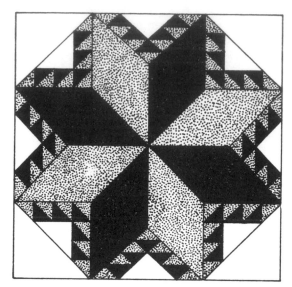

Lucinda's Star

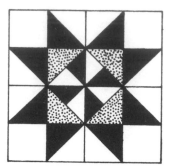

Martha Washington Star

Many-pointed Star

Mexican Rose
Mexican Star, Var. 1

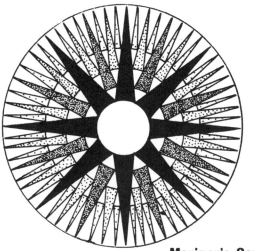

Mariner's Compass
Rising Sun, Var. 1

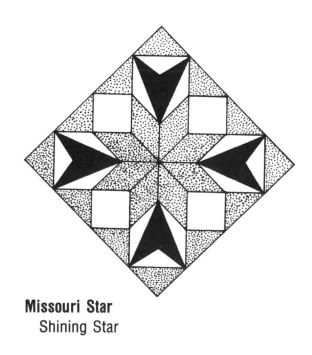

Missouri Star
Shining Star

Modern Star

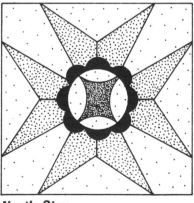

Morning Star   Variation 3

Northern Lights
   Blazing Star, Var. 3
   Four-Pointed Star
   Star, Var. 2

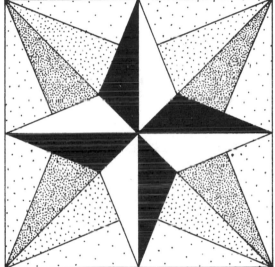

Morning Star   Variation 1

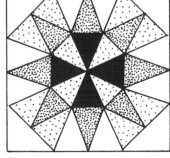

Morning Star   Variation 2

North Star
Star Tulip, Var. 2

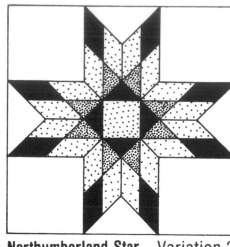

Northumberland Star   Variation 2

Odd Fellows' Cross   Variation 1

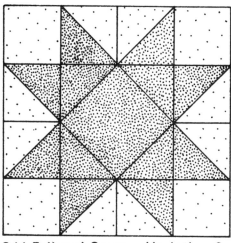

Odd Fellows' Cross   Variation 2

Odd Star

Ohio Star   Variation 1
   Lone Star, Var. 1
   Old Tippecanoe and Tyler Too
   Variable Star

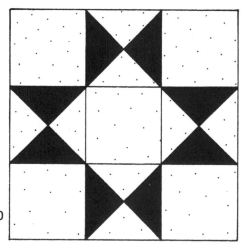

Ohio Star   Variation 2
   Eastern Star, Var. 1
   Eight-Point Star
   Lone Star, Var. 2
   Lucky Star
   Shoofly, Var. 2
   Texas
   Tippecanoe and Tyler Too

Oklahoma Star
Rising Sun, Var. 2

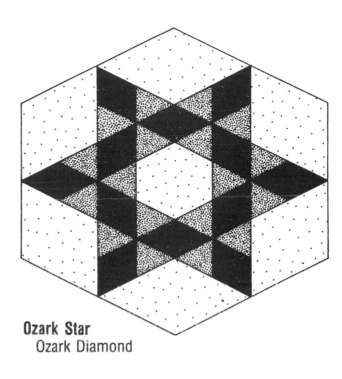

Ozark Star
Ozark Diamond

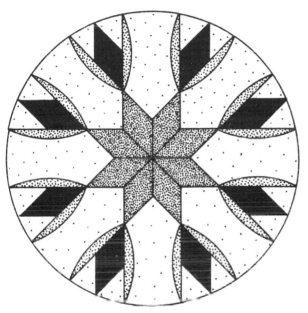

Olive's Yellow Tulip

Patty's Star

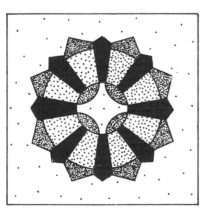

Oriental Star   Variation 1

Persian Star

Pieced Star Variation 1
Pierced Star

Pointing Star

Philippines

Pontiac Star

Purple Cross

Prairie Queen
Variation 2

Prairie Star
  Harvest Star
  Harvest Sun
  Ship's Wheel

Queen of the May

Ring Around the Star
  Rolling Star, Var. 2
  Star and Chains

19

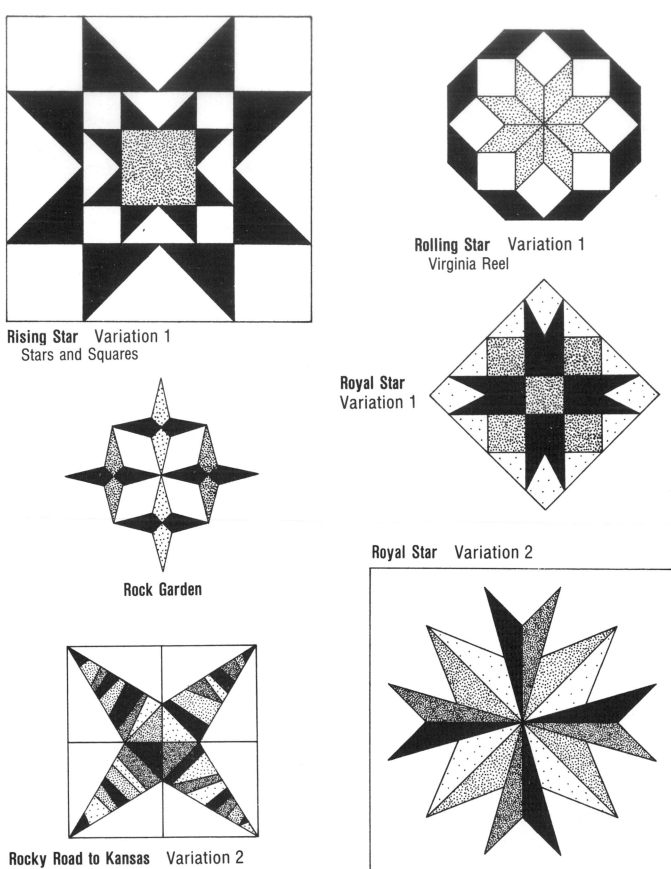

Rising Star   Variation 1
Stars and Squares

Rolling Star   Variation 1
Virginia Reel

Royal Star
Variation 1

Rock Garden

Royal Star   Variation 2

Rocky Road to Kansas   Variation 2

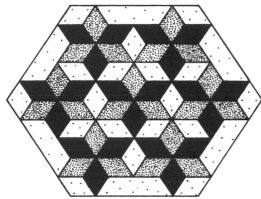

Seven Sisters
Evening Star, Var. 4

Slashed Star
Sunflower

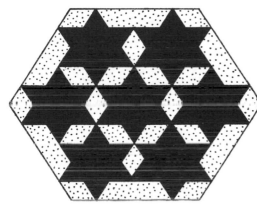

Seven Stars
Boutonnlere

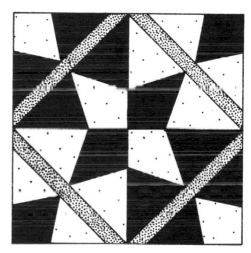

Small Business

Sky Rocket

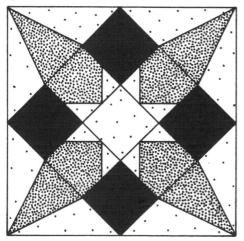

Spiderweb
Variation 2

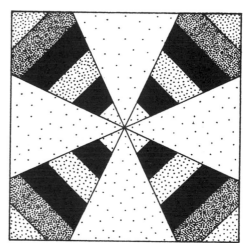

Spiderweb
Variation 3

Star and Crescent
Variation 2
Star of the Four Winds

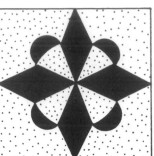

Star   Variation 1

Star and Cross
Variation 1

Star and Cone

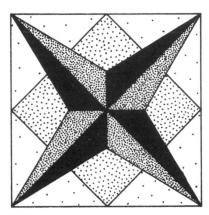

Star and Hexagon
Tiny Star

Star and Crescent
Variation 1
Flower Star, Var. 2
Twinkling Star, Var. 2

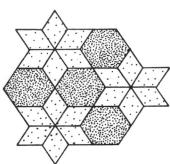

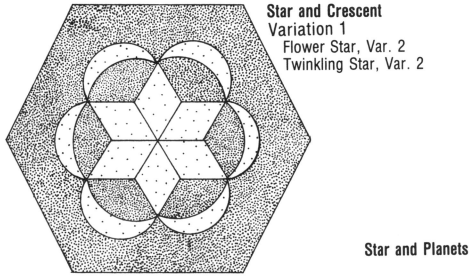

Star and Planets

Star Flower
Variation 2

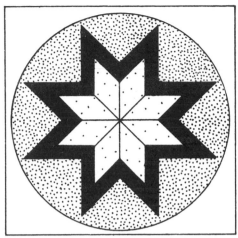

Star of Hope
Variation 2

Starlight   Variation 1

Star of Le Moyne   Variation 1
    Brunswick Star, Var. 2
    Eight-Pointed Star,
      Var. 1
    Lemon Star, Var. 1
    LeMoyne Star, Var. 1
    Star of the East, Var. 1
    Star of LeMoine, Var. 1

Starlight
Variation 2

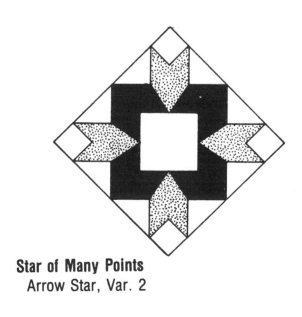

Star of Many Points
Arrow Star, Var. 2

23

Star of the West
Variation 2

Star of North Carolina
North Carolina Star

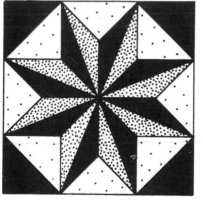

Star of the East Variation 3
Silver and Gold

St. Louis Star

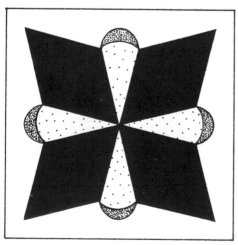

Star of the West
Variation 1
    Compass, Var. 1
    Four Birds
    Four Winds
    King's Star, Var. 2

Star Tulip
Variation 1

Sunburst
Variation 1

Star Within a Star
Carpenter's Wheel, Var. 1
Double Star
Star of the East, Var. 2

String Quilt

Sunburst   Variation 2

Sunbeam

Sunburst   Variation 3

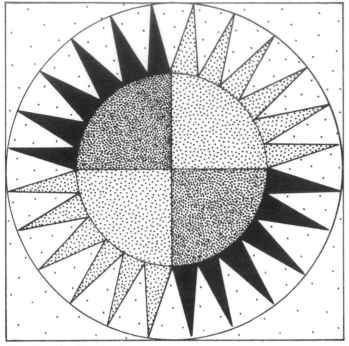

Sunburst   Variation 4

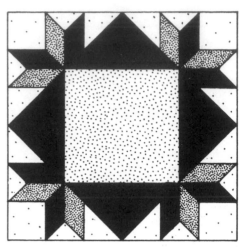

Swallows in a Window

Tennessee Star

Tangled Cobwebs

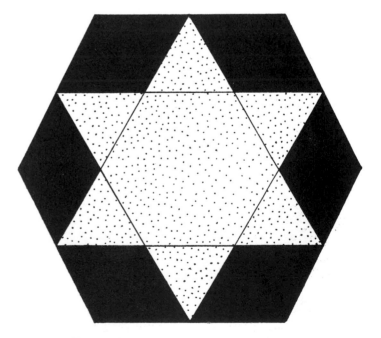

Texas Star

Union Star

Yankee Pride
Maple Leaf, Var. 3

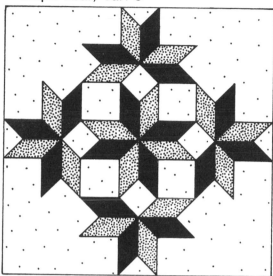

Virginia Star
Eastern Star, Var. 2
Star upon Stars
Virginia's Star

SUPPLEMENT

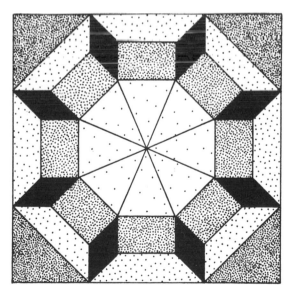

Castle Wall

World Without End
Amethyst
Golden Wedding Ring
Windmill Star

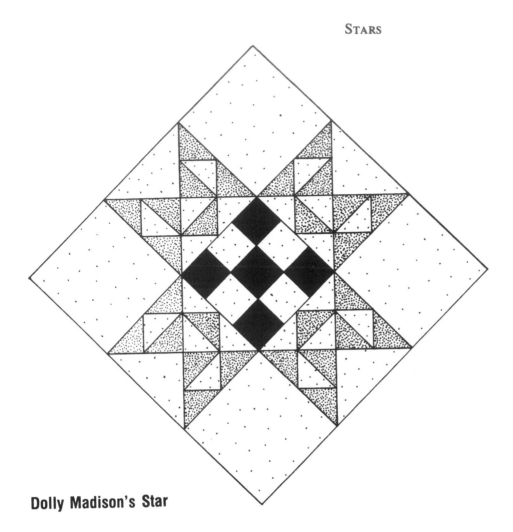

Dolly Madison's Star

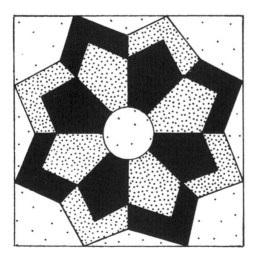

Eight-Pointed Star Variation 3

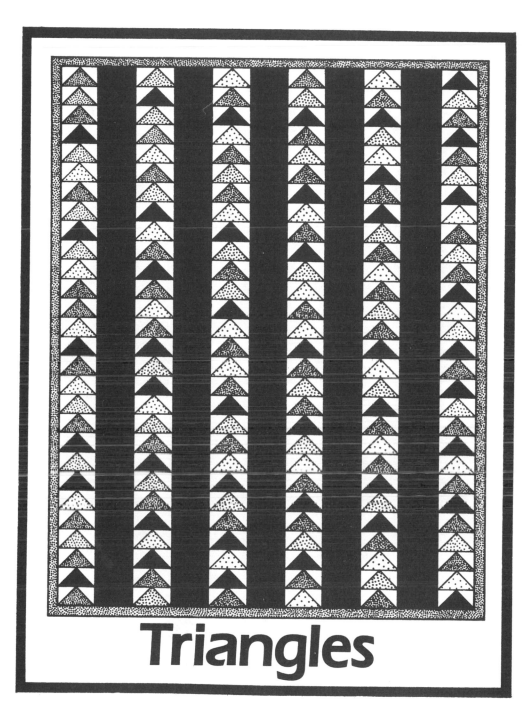

Triangles

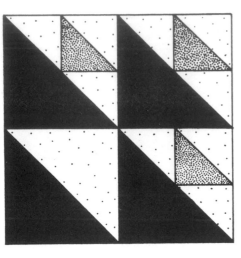

Aircraft

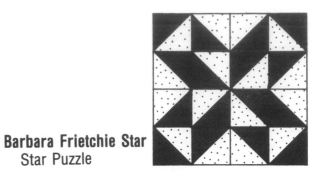

Barbara Frietchie Star
Star Puzzle

Album
Variation 4

Barn Raising

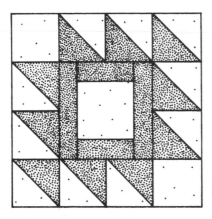

Album
Variation 5

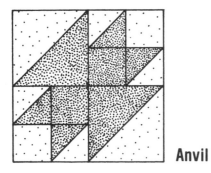

Anvil

Barrister's Block
Lawyer's Puzzle

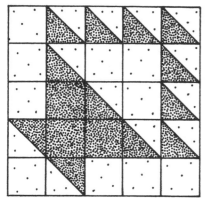

Basket of Triangles
Fruit Basket, Var. 2

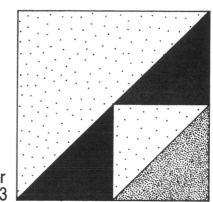

Birds in Air
Variation 3

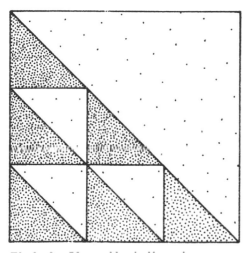

Birds in Air Variation 1
Flying Birds
Flying Geese, Var. 1
Flock of Geese

Blindman's Fancy

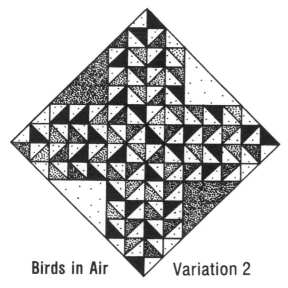

Birds in Air Variation 2

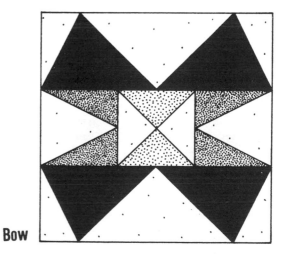

Bow

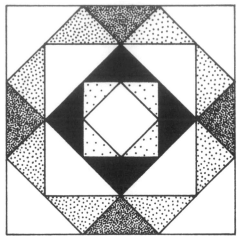

Boxes
Variation 2

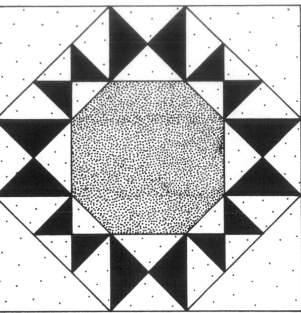

Buttons and Bows
Wheel of Fortune, Var. 3

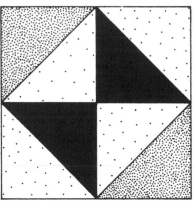

Broken Dishes

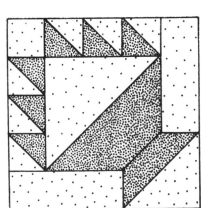

Cactus Flower

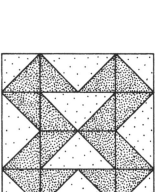

Brown Goose
    Brown
    Devil's Claws, Var. 1
    Double Z
    Grey Goose

Cakestand

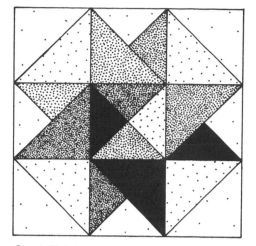

Card Trick

Century
Variation 2

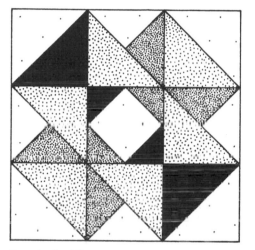

Castle in Air

Cherry Basket Variation 1
Flower Basket

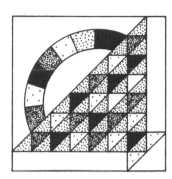

Cherry Basket
Variation 2

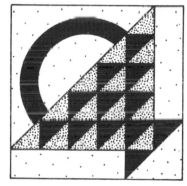

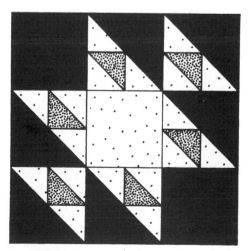

Cat's Cradle

Christmas Tree
Tree of Life, Var. 3

Crazy Ann Variation 1
Follow the Leader
Twist and Turn

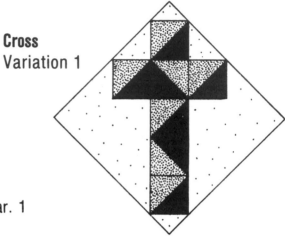

Cross
Variation 1

Corn and Beans
Variation 2
    Duck and Duckling
    Handy Andy, Var. 4
    Hen and Chickens, Var. 1
    Shoofly, Var. 4

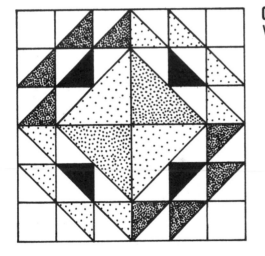

City Square
London Square

Crossed Canoes
Tippecanoe

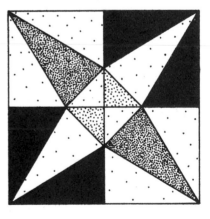

Cotton Reel

Crosses and Losses
    Double X, Var. 2
    Fox and Geese
    Old Maid's Puzzle
    X

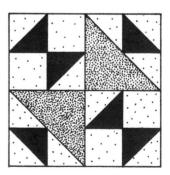

Double Pyramid

Dove in the Window   Variation 1

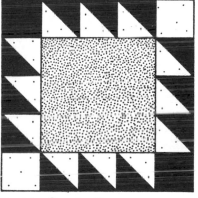

Double Sawtooth

Duck and Ducklings
  Corn and Beans, Var. 1
  Handy Andy, Var. 5
  Hens and Chickens, Var. 1
  Shoofly, Var. 3
  Wild Goose Chase, Var. 2

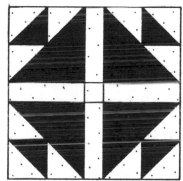

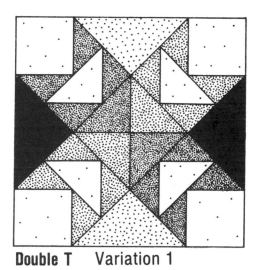

Double T   Variation 1

Dutchman's Puzzle
Dutch Windmill

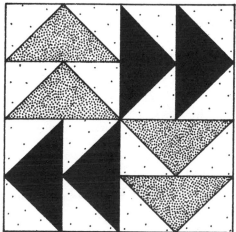

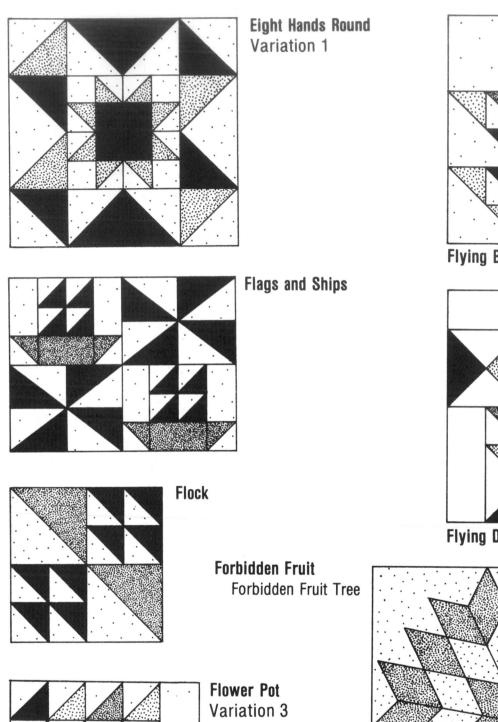

Eight Hands Round
Variation 1

Flags and Ships

Flock

Forbidden Fruit
Forbidden Fruit Tree

Flower Pot
Variation 3

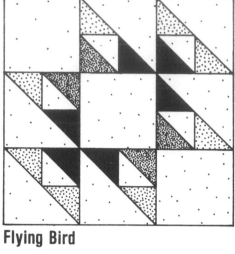

Flying Bird

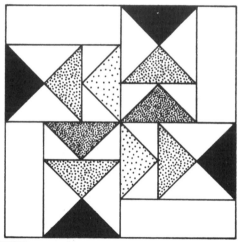

Flying Dutchman Variation 3

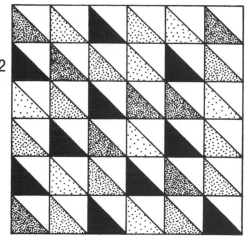

Geese in Flight
   Battlegrounds
   Indian Trails, Var. 2
   Rambling Road, Var. 2
   Soldiers March
   Storm at Sea, Var. 3

Four Ts
   Mixed T

Four X

Georgetown Circles

Fruit Basket   Variation 1

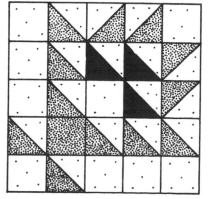

Golden Stairs

Goose in the Pond
Variation 1

Grandmother's Favorite

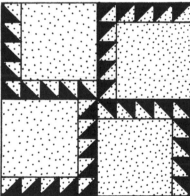

Grandmother's Pinwheel

Grape Basket

Gretchen

Handy Andy Variation 1
Gentleman's Fancy

Hill and Valley

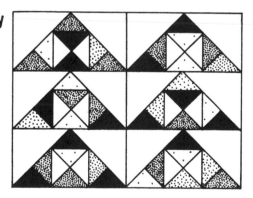

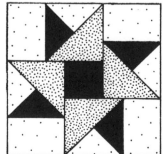

Hope of Hartford

Hovering Birds

Ice Cream Bowl

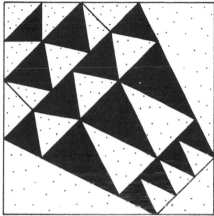

Indian Trails
Variation 1

Bear's Paw, Var. 2   Rambling Road, Var. 1
Climbing Rose   Rambling Rose
Flying Dutchman, Var. 2   Storm at Sea, Var. 1
Forest Path   Tangled Tares
Irish Puzzle   Weather Vane, Var. 1
Kansas Trouble, Var. 1   Winding Walk
North Wind, Var. 1
Old Maid's Ramble, Var. 1
Prickly Pear, Var. 2

Indian Meadows
Variation 2
    Queen Charlotte's Crown, Var. 2

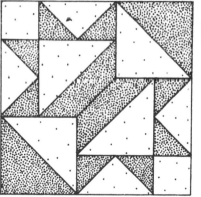

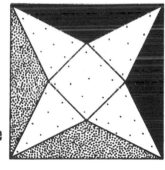

Kaleidoscope
Variation 2

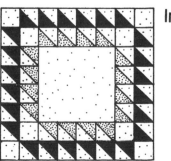

Indian Plumes

Kaleidoscope
Variation 3

Kansas Trouble   Variation 2

Lost Ships   Variation 1
  Lady of the Lake, Var. 2
  Rockly Glen, Var. 2

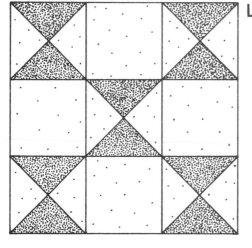

Letter X
  Clown's Choice
  Flying X

Maltese Cross
Variation 1

Lightning Strips
  Chevron
  Rail Fence
  Snake Fence, Var. 1
  Streak of Lightning
  Zigzag, Var. 1
  1,000 Pyramids

Maryland Beauty

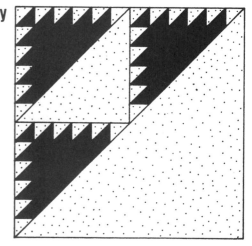

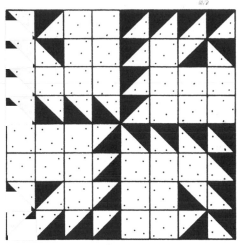

Merry Go Round

New York Beauty   Variation 2
Rocky Mountain Road

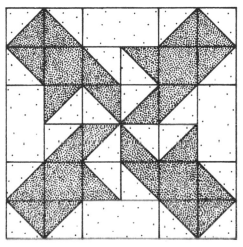

Mrs. Morgan's Choice

Next-door Neighbor

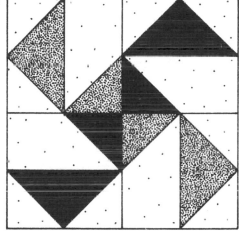

New York Beauty
Variation 1

Night and Day

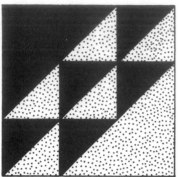

North Wind
Variation 2

Odd Fellows' Chain

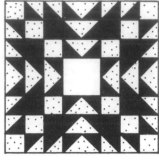

Ocean Waves
Variation 1

Old Maid's Ramble
Variation 2
    Lady of the Lake,
      Var. 1

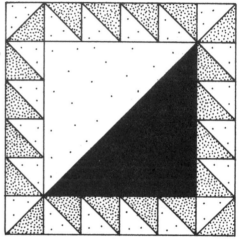

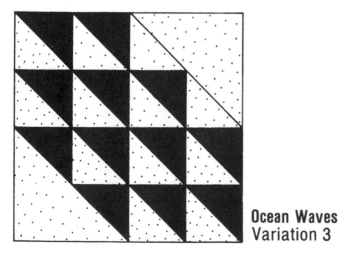

Ocean Waves
Variation 2

Old Maid's Ramble Variation 3
    Crimson Rambler
    Rambler
    Spring Beauty

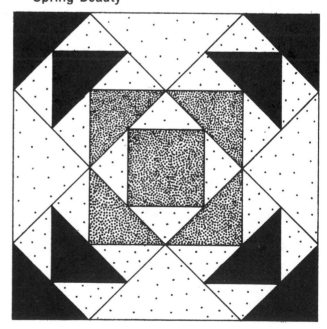

Ocean Waves
Variation 3

Old Maid's Ramble
Variation 4
  Lady of the Lake, Var. 3

Path Through the Woods

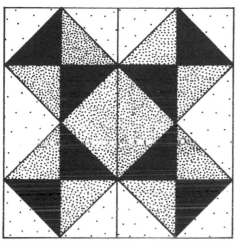

Old Tippecanoe

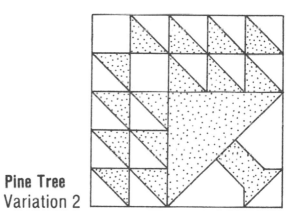

Pine Tree
Variation 2

Palm Leaves Hosannah!
  Hosanna
  Palm
  Palm Leaf, Var. 1

Pine Tree   Variation 3
  Temperance Tree

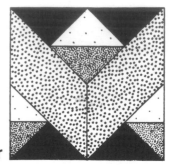

Ribbon Border

Pine Tree
Variation 4

Ribbons

Pinwheel Star

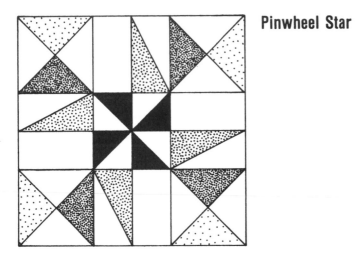

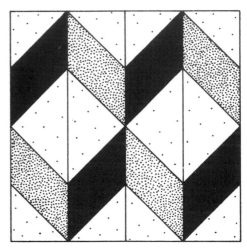

Railroad Crossing
Variation 1

Rolling Pinwheel
Variation 1

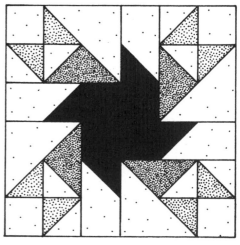

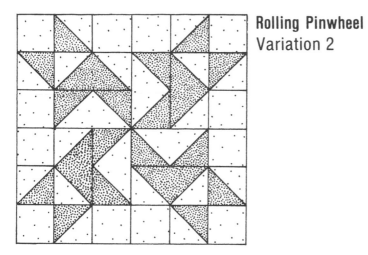

**Rolling Pinwheel
Variation 2**

Sailboats

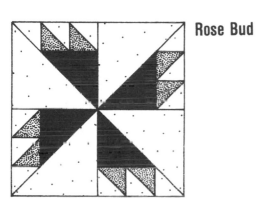

Rose Bud

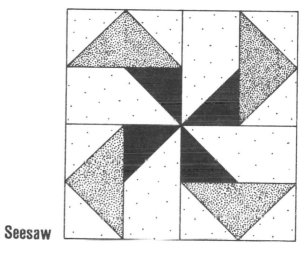

Seesaw

Sailboat

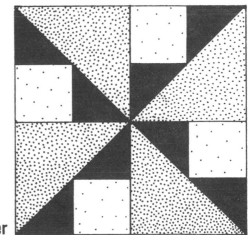

Spinner

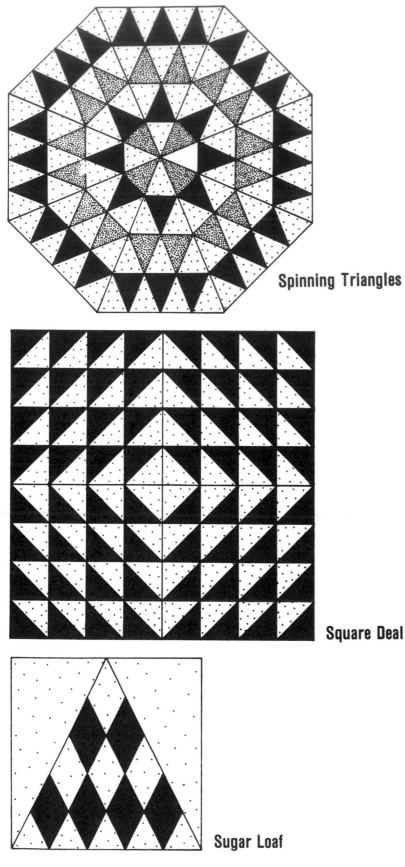

Spinning Triangles

Square Deal

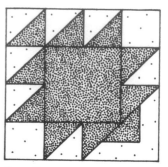

Swallow

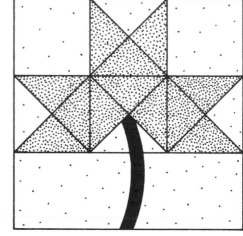

Sweet Gum Leaf

Sugar Loaf

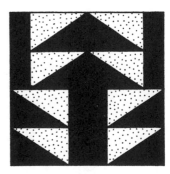

Tall Pine Tree

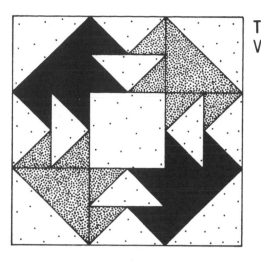

T-Blocks
Variation 1
   Capital T
   Double-T, Var. 2

Thousand Pyramids
  Pyramids
  Triangles

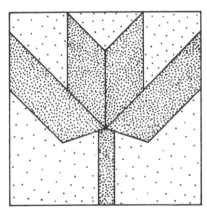

Tea Leaf
Variation 1

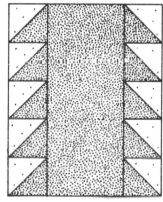

Tree of Life
Variation 2

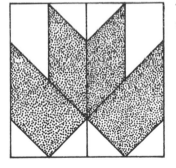

Tea Leaf
Variation 2

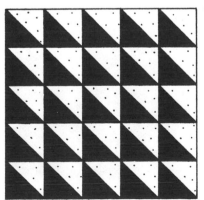

Tents of Armageddon

Tree of Paradise
Variation 1

47

Tree of Paradise
Variation 2

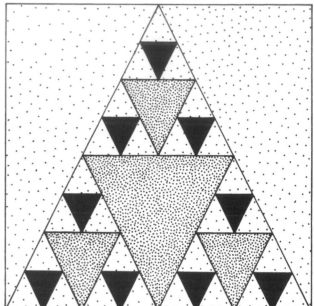

Triangular Triangles

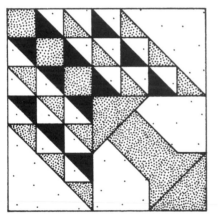

Tree of Paradise
Variation 3

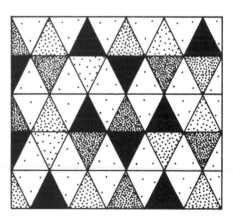

Tumblers
Variation 1

Triangle Puzzle

Twenty-four Triangles

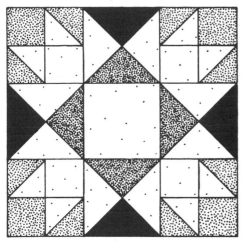

Union Squares

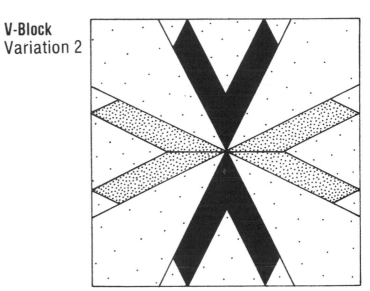

V-Block
Variation 2

Unknown Four-Patch

Water Wheel
Variation 2
Whirlwind

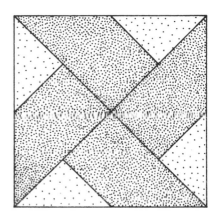

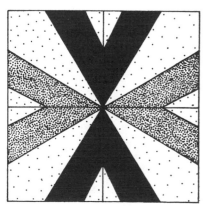

V-Block   Variation 1

Whirligig
Variation 2

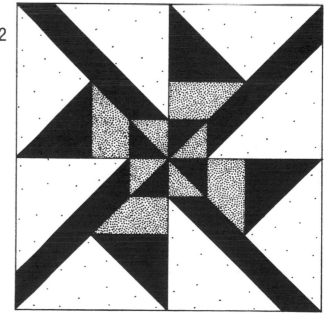

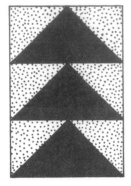

Wild Goose Chase
Variation 1

Windmill Variation 1
  Crow's Foot, Var. 3
  Fan Mill, Var. 1
  Flutter Wheels, Var. 1
  Fly, Var. 1
  Honey's Choice
  Kathy's Ramble, Var. 1
  Mill Wheel, Var. 1
  Old Windmill
  Pinwheel, Var. 1
  Slash Diagonal
  Sugar Bowl, Var. 1
  Water Mill
  Water Wheel, Var. 1

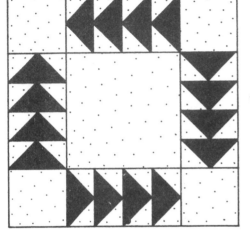

Wild Goose Chase
Variation 4

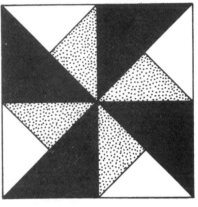

Windmill
Variation 4

Wild Goose Chase
Variation 5

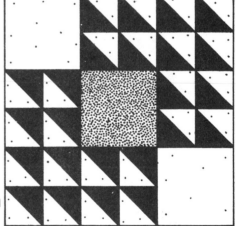

Winged Square
Variation 1
  Cut Glass Dish
  Golden Gates

Windblown Square
  Balkan Puzzle
  Zigzag Tile

Yankee Puzzle
Variation 1
  Hourglass, Var. 2

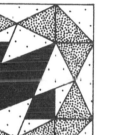

Yankee Puzzle
Variation 2

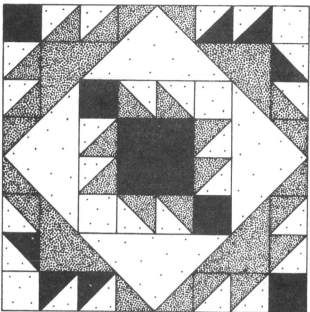

Indian Hatchet   Variation 3

SUPPLEMENT

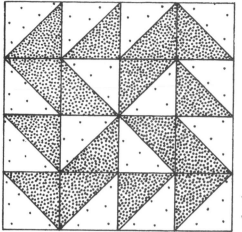

Dove in the Window   Variation 3

Rocky Glen
Variation 4
Lost Ships,
Var. 2

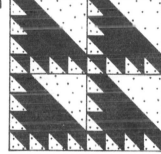

**Free Trade
Block**

Sawtooth
Variation 2

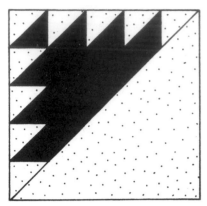

Sawtooth
Variation 4

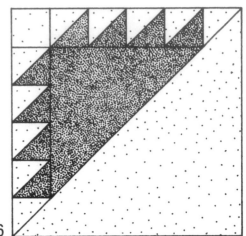

Sawtooth
Variation 6

Circles

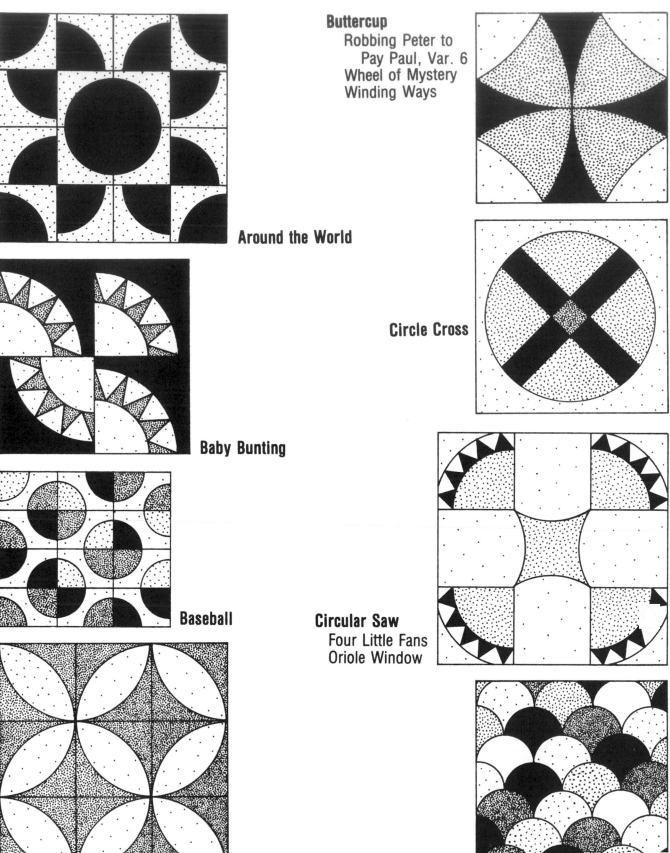

Buttercup
Robbing Peter to
Pay Paul, Var. 6
Wheel of Mystery
Winding Ways

Around the World

Baby Bunting

Baseball

Bay Leaf

Circle Cross

Circular Saw
Four Little Fans
Oriole Window

Clamshell

Country Crossroads

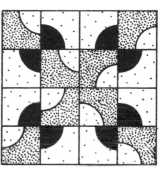

Dresden Plate   Variation 3

Crossroads

Drunkard's Path
Variation 1
  Country Husband
  Solomon's Puzzle
  World's Puzzle

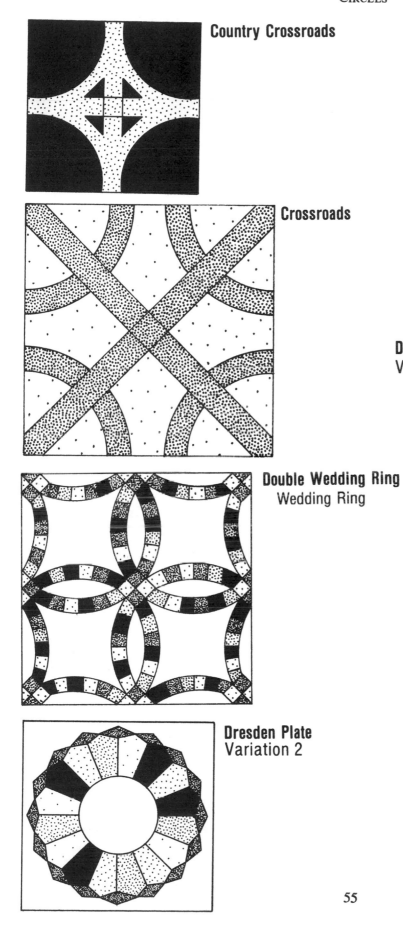

Double Wedding Ring
Wedding Ring

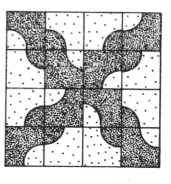

Drunkard's Path
Variation 2

Dresden Plate
Variation 2

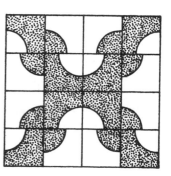

Drunkard's Path
Variation 3
  Falling Timber

Drunkard's Path Variation 4

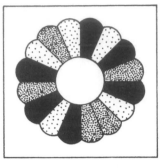

Friendship Ring
Aster
Dresden Plate,
   Var. 1

Flo's Fan

Full-blown Tulip
Variation 2

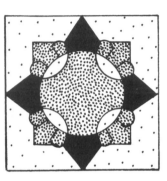

Fool's Puzzle
Variation 1

Grandmother's Fan
Fan
Fanny's Fan, Var. 1

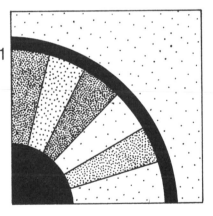

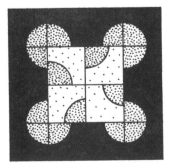

Fool's Puzzle
Variation 2

Hearts and Gizzards
Lazy Daisy, Var. 1
Petal Quilt
Pierrot's Pom-pon
Springtime Blossom
Wheel of Fortune, Var. 1
Windmill, Var. 2

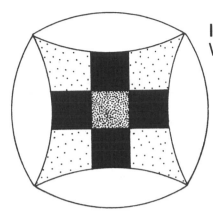

Improved Nine-patch
Variation 1
   Bailey Nine-Patch
   Glorified Nine-Patch

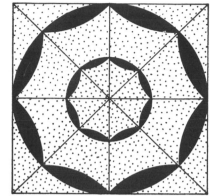

Odds and Ends

Lafayette Orange Peel
   Melon Patch
   Orange Peel, Var. 2

Love Ring
   Lone Ring
   Nonesuch

Orange Peel
Variation 1

   Compass, Var. 2
   Dolly Madison's Workbox, Var. 2
   Robbing Peter to Pay Paul, Var. 4

Missouri Beauty

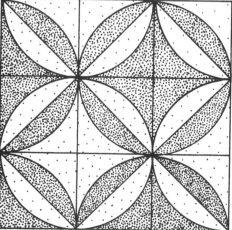

Orange Peel
Variation 3
   Dolly Madison's Workbox, Var. 1
   Rob Peter to Pay Paul, Var. 2

Pickle Dish
Indian Summer
Indian Wedding Ring

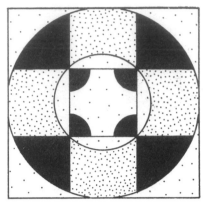

Queen's Crown
Variation 2

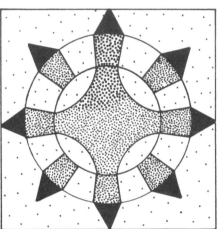

Pilot's Wheel

Queen's Pride

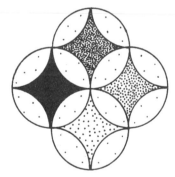

Pincushion
Cathedral Window

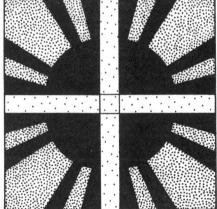

Rebecca's Fan

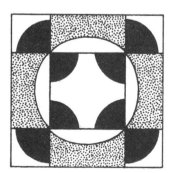

Queen's Crown
Variation 1

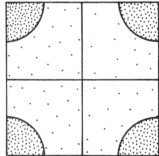

Reverse Baseball

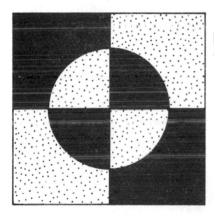

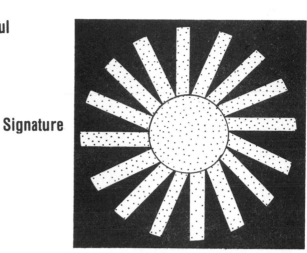

Robbing Peter to Pay Paul
Variation 2

Robbing Peter to Pay Paul
Variation 3
    Falling Timbers
    Vine of Friendship

Signature

Snowball Variation 1
    Mill Wheel, Var. 2
    Old Mill Wheel
    Pullman Puzzle

Rob Peter to Pay Paul
Variation 1

Snowball Variation 2
Compass, Var. 3

Rocky Road to Dublin

Snowball
Variation 4

Snowball Wreath

Steeplechase
Bows and Arrows

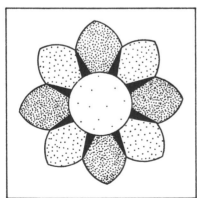

Spools
Always Friends
Friendship Chain

Strawberry
Full-Blown Tulip, Var. 1
Oriental Star, Var. 2

Turkey Tracks
Variation 1
Wandering Foot

Star Flower Variation 1
Golden Glow, Var. 1

Unnamed
Variation 1

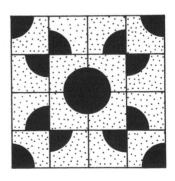

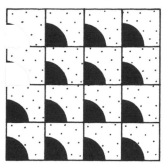

Unnamed Variation 2

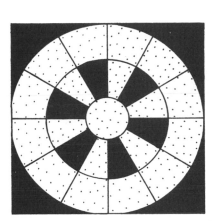

Wheel of Fortune Variation 4

Victoria's Crown

Wheel of Fortune Variation 5

Wheel of Chance
  True Lover's Buggy Wheel

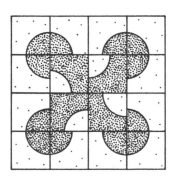

Wonder of the World

SUPPLEMENT

Reel

Combinations

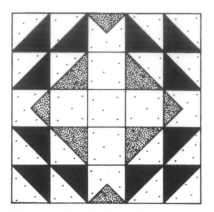

Album Variation 1

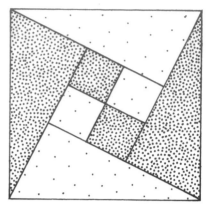

Arabic Lattice

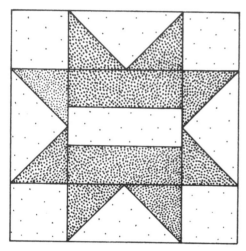

Album Variation 2

Arrowheads Variation 1

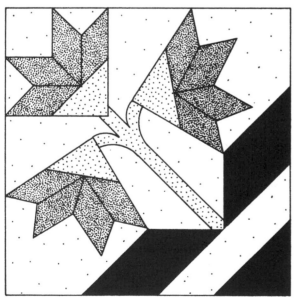

Antique Shop Tulip
Double Tulip

Aunt Sukey's Choice
Puss 'n' Boots

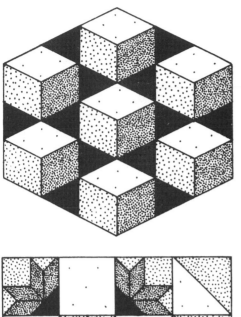

Baby Blocks
Variation 2

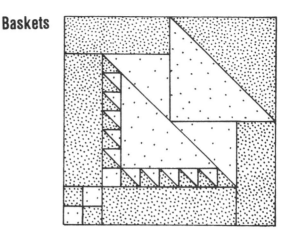

Baskets

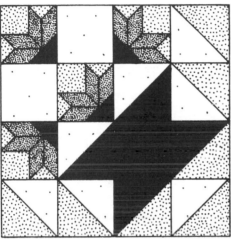

Bear Tracks Variation 1
 Bear's Foot
 Bear's Paw, Var. 3
 Bear's Track, Var. 1
 Cross and Crown, Var. 3
 Duck's Foot in the Mud,
  Var. 2
 Goose Tracks, Var. 1
 Hand of Friendship, Var. 2

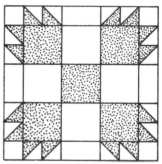

Illinois Turkey Track
Lily Design

Basket of Lillies
Variation 2
 Basket of Tulips, Var. 2

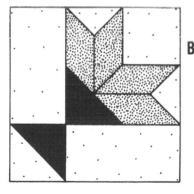

Basket of Scraps
 Cactus Basket, Var. 2
 Desert Rose, Var. 2
 Texas Rose, Var. 2
 Texas Treasure, Var. 2

Bear Tracks
Variation 2
 Bear's Track, Var. 2

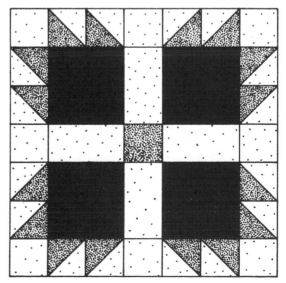

Basket of Tulips
Variation 1
 Basket of Lilies, Var. 1

Beggar's Block
Cats and Mice, Var. 2

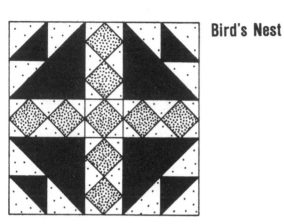

Bird's Nest

Bow Knot
Farmer's Puzzle
Swastika, Var. 1

Blackford's Beauty

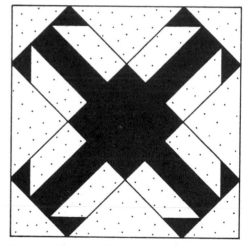

Boxed Ts

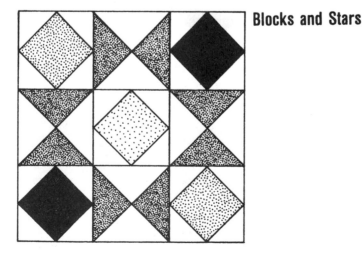

Blocks and Stars

Braced Star

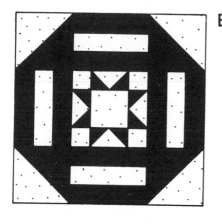

Burnham Square

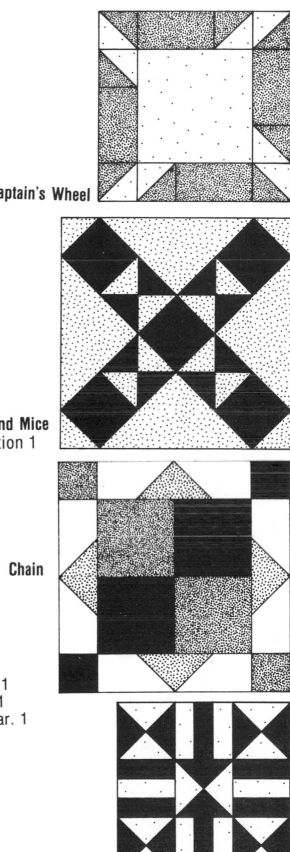

Captain's Wheel

Cats and Mice
Variation 1

Chain

Chain and Hourglass

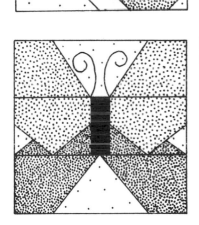

Butterfly
Variation 1

Butterfly
Variation 2

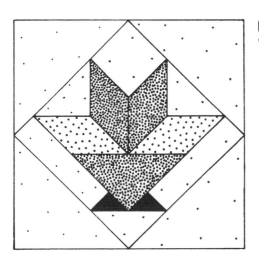

Cactus Basket
Variation 1
    Desert Rose, Var. 1
    Texas Rose, Var. 1
    Texas Treasure, Var. 1

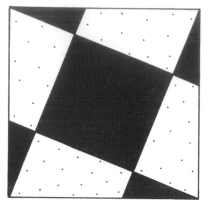

Checkerboard Skew

Children of Israel

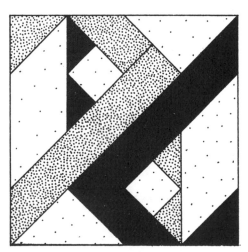

Chinese Puzzle   Variation 1

Christmas Star
Variation 2

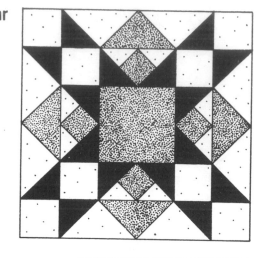

Churn Dash Variation 1
 Lover's Knot
 Monkey Wrench, Var. 1

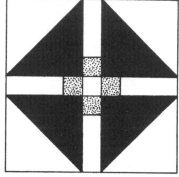

Churn Dash
Variation 2

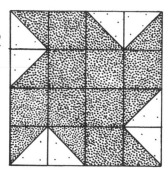

Claws

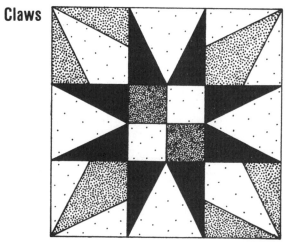

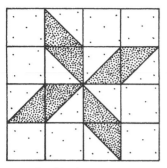

Clay's Choice
Harry's Star
Henry of the West
Jackson's Star, Var. 2
Star of the West, Var. 3

Crazy Ann   Variation 2

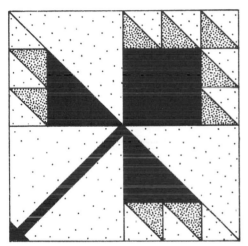

Clover Blossom
English Ivy

Crazy House

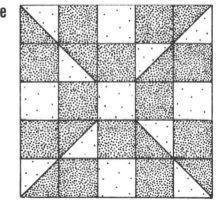

Combination Star
Ornate Star

Cross and Crown
Variation 1

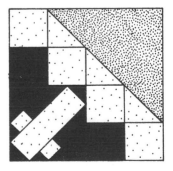

69

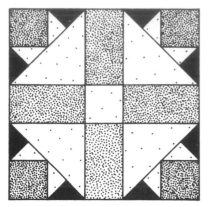

Cross and Crown   Variation 4

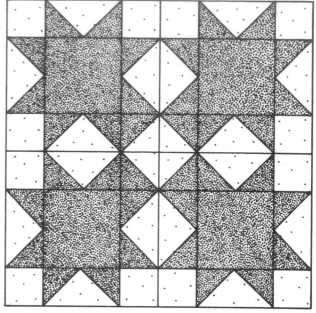

Crow Foot
Devil's Claws,
Var. 2

Cross Upon a Cross

Cross and Crown, Var. 2
Crown and Cross
Crowned Cross, Var. 1
Golgotha, Var. 2
Three Crosses, Var. 2

Crown and Thorns
Crown of Thorns
Georgetown Circle, Var. 1
Memory Wreath
Single Wedding Ring,
    Var. 1

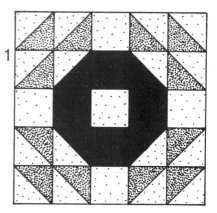

Crow's Foot
Variation 4

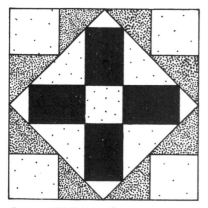

Cross Within a Cross

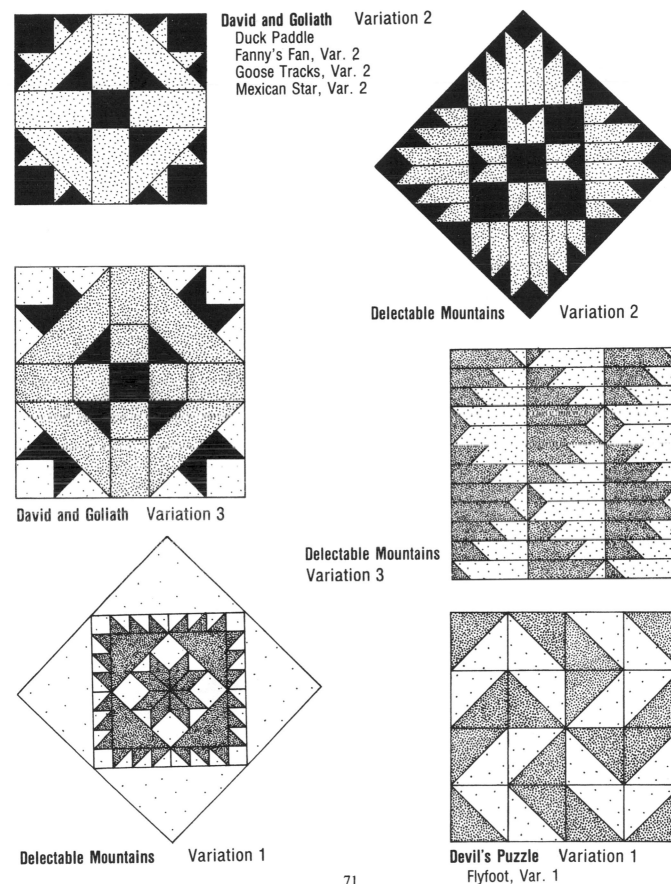

David and Goliath Variation 2
Duck Paddle
Fanny's Fan, Var. 2
Goose Tracks, Var. 2
Mexican Star, Var. 2

Delectable Mountains Variation 2

David and Goliath Variation 3

Delectable Mountains
Variation 3

Delectable Mountains Variation 1

Devil's Puzzle Variation 1
Flyfoot, Var. 1

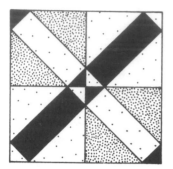

Devil's Puzzle   Variation 2
Flyfoot, Var. 2

Double Square
Variation 1

Dogwood Blossoms

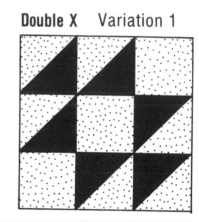

Double X   Variation 1

Domino and Squares

Dove in the Window   Variation 2

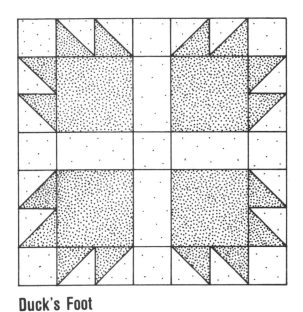

Duck's Foot

Duck's Foot in the Mud
Variation 1
   Bear's Paw, Var. 1
   Crow's Foot, Var. 1
   Hand of Friendship, Var. 1

Dusty Miller

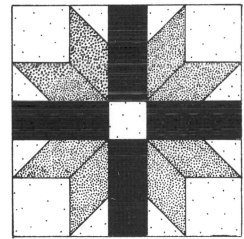

Dutch Mill

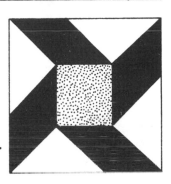

Eccentric Star
Variation 1

E-Z Quilt

Fannie's Fan
Variation 1

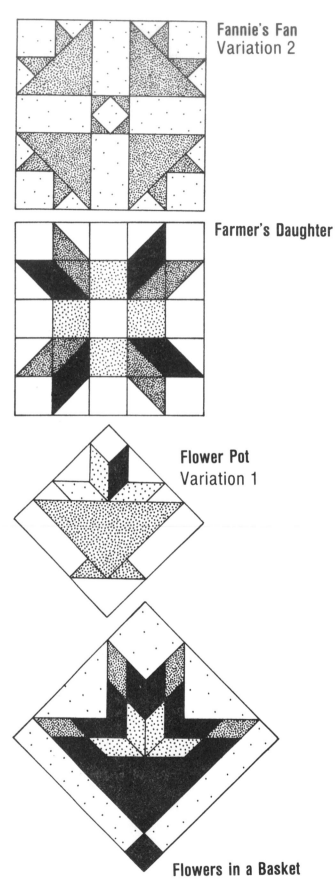

Fannie's Fan
Variation 2

Farmer's Daughter

Flower Pot
Variation 1

Flowers in a Basket

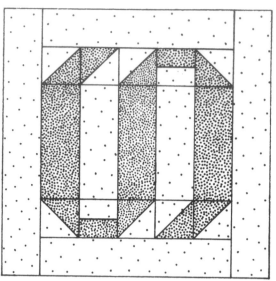

Flowing Ribbon

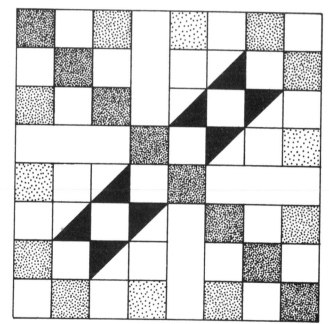

Flying Clouds   Variation 1
Four Frogs

Flying Clouds
Variation 2

74

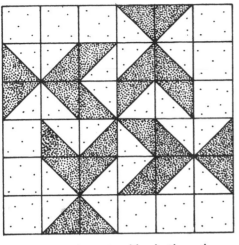

Flying Dutchman   Variation 1

Four Little Baskets

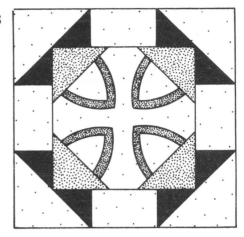

Flying Geese   Variation 2
Handy Andy, Var. 6

Friendship Knot

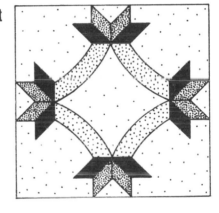

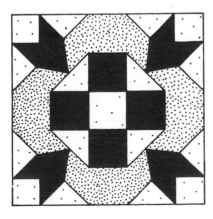

Four Darts
　　Bull's Eye
　　David and Goliath, Var. 1
　　Doe and Darts
　　Flying Darts

Garden of Eden   Variation 1

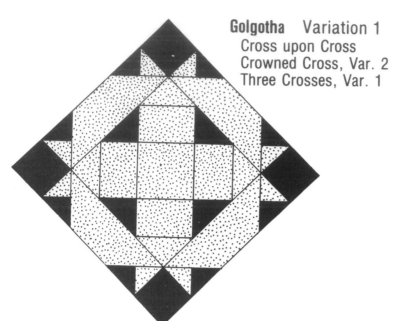

Golgotha   Variation 1
Cross upon Cross
Crowned Cross, Var. 2
Three Crosses, Var. 1

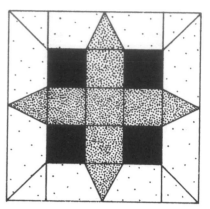

Grandmother's Cross

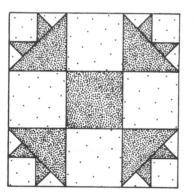

Goose Tracks
Variation 3

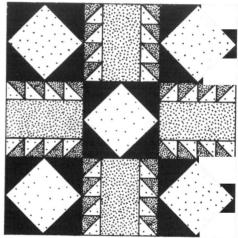

Grandmother's Dream
Mother's Dream

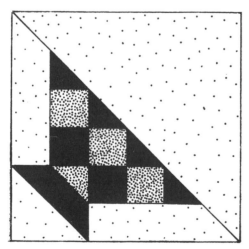

Grandmother's Basket

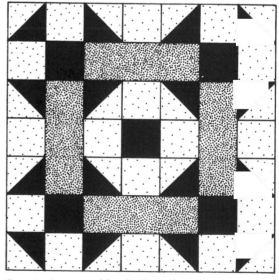

Greek Cross   Variation 2

76

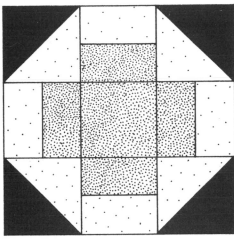

Greek Cross   Variation 3
Grecian
Grecian Design

Hayes' Corner

Heart's Desire

Handy Andy   Variation 2

Hen and Chickens
Variation 2

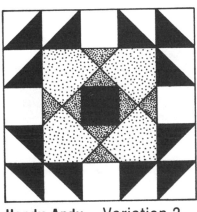

Handy Andy   Variation 3

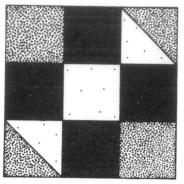

Hourglass   Variation 1

Indian Hatchet
Variation 2

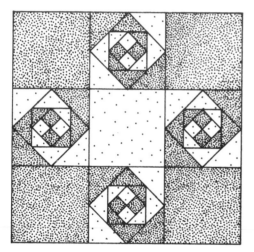

Indiana Puzzle
Monkey Wrench, Var. 3

Indian Meadows Variation 1
Mountain Meadows
Queen Charlotte's Crown,
Var. 1

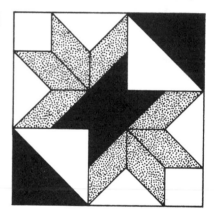

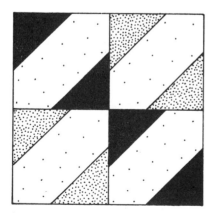

Indian Hatchet   Variation 1

Irish Chain
Variation 1

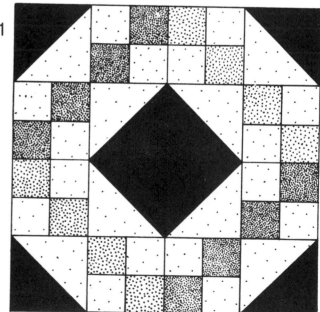

78

Jack in the Box
Whirligig, Var. 1

Joseph's Coat   Variation 1
Scrap-Bag

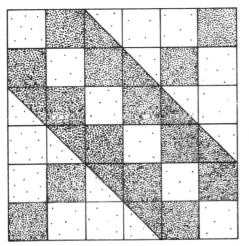

Jacob's Ladder   Variation 1

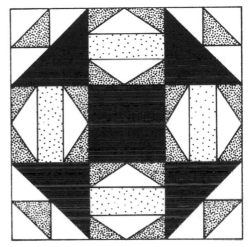

Joseph's Coat   Variation 2
Mollie's Choice

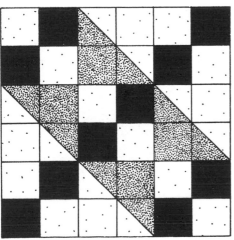

Jacob's Ladder   Variation 2
   Road to California, Var. 1
   Rocky Road to California
   Stepping Stones, Var. 1
   Tail of Benjamin's Kite
   Trail of the Covered Wagon
   Underground Railroad
   Wagon Tracks

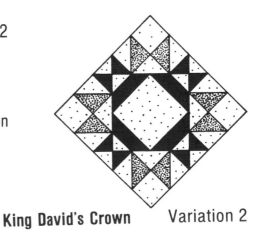

King David's Crown   Variation 2

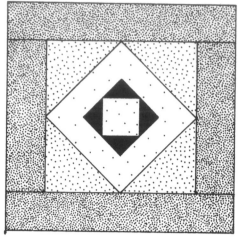

King's Crown Variation 1

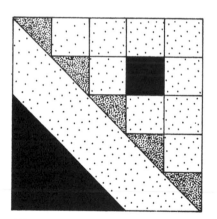

King's Crown Variation 2
Greek Cross, Var. 1

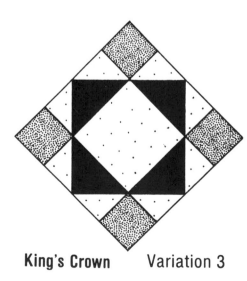

King's Crown Variation 3

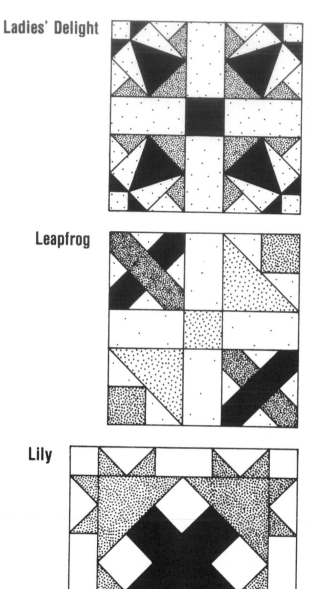

Ladies' Delight

Leapfrog

Lily

Lily of the Field

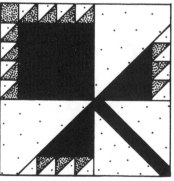

Little Giant

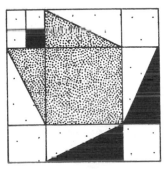

Magnolia Bud

Maple Leaf   Variation 1

Maple Leaf
Variation 2
  Palm Leaf, Var. 2
  Poplar Leaf

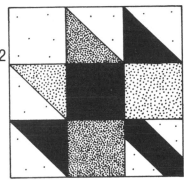

Mare's Nest

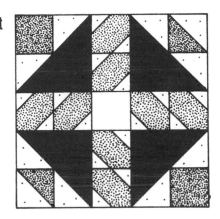

Mary Tenney Gray Travel Club Patch

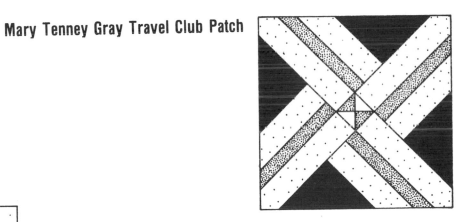

Memory Block

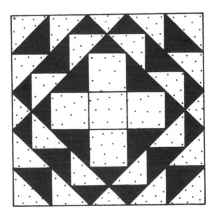

81

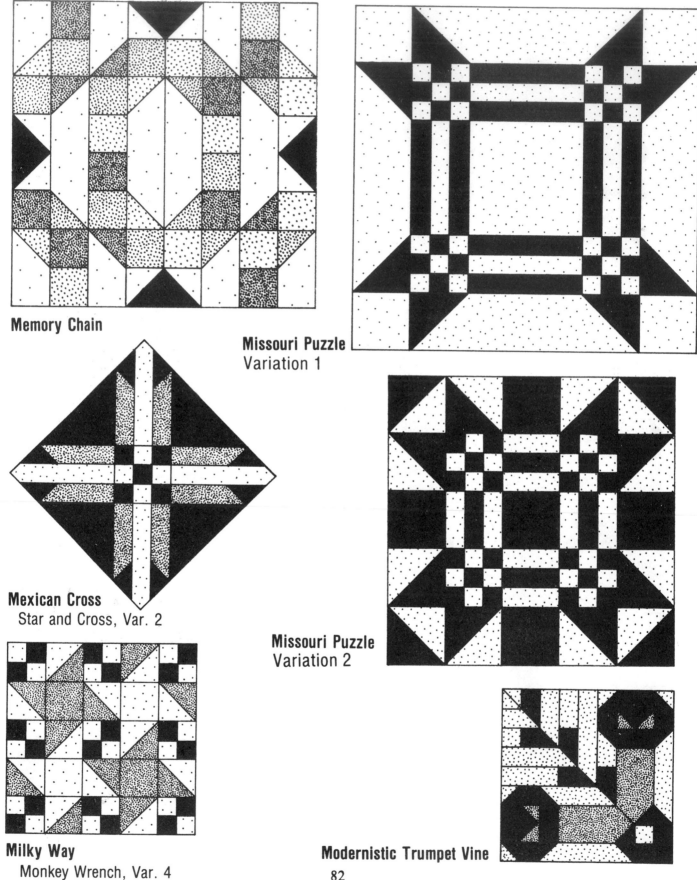

Memory Chain

Missouri Puzzle
Variation 1

Mexican Cross
Star and Cross, Var. 2

Missouri Puzzle
Variation 2

Milky Way
Monkey Wrench, Var. 4

Modernistic Trumpet Vine

82

Mother's Fancy Star

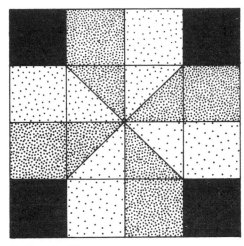

Nelson's Victory

Mrs. Cleveland's Choice
County Fair

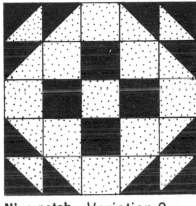

Nine-patch   Variation 2

Necktie
Variation 2

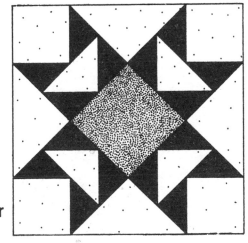

Northumberland Star
Variation 1

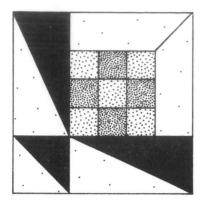

Nosegay Variation 2

Philadelphia Pavement

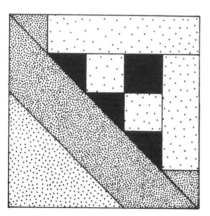

Old King Cole's Crown

Pieced Pyramids

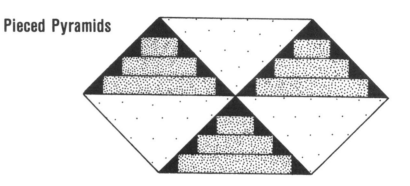

Pieced Star Variation 2
Octagonal Star, Var. 2

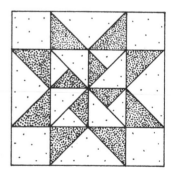

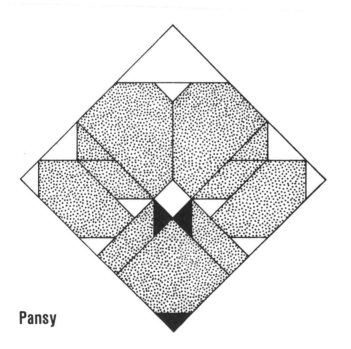

Pansy

Pigeon Toes

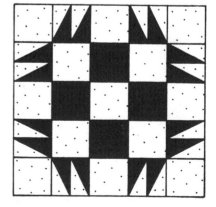

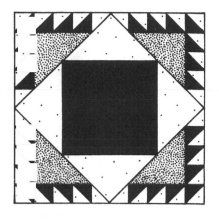

Pine Burr

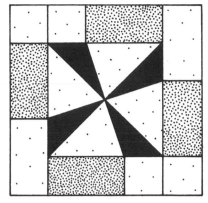

Pinwheel Skew

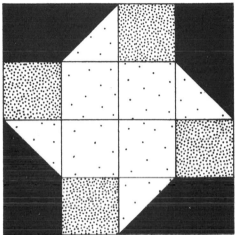

Pinwheel Variation 2
  Crow's Foot, Var. 2
  Fan Mill, Var. 2
  Flutter Wheels, Var. 2
  Fly, Var. 2
  Foot
  Kathy's Ramble, Var. 2
  Sugar Bowl, Var. 2

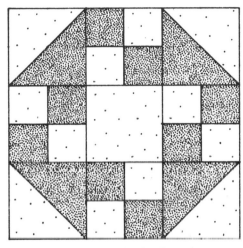

Prairie Queen Variation 1

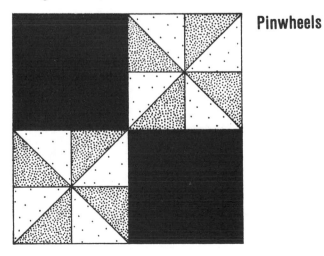

Pinwheels

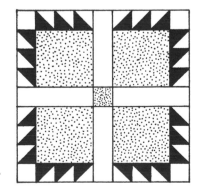

Premium Star

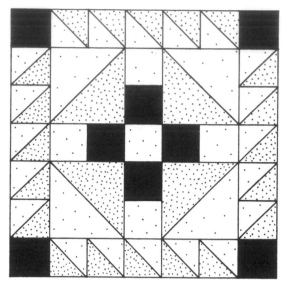

Prickly Pear Variation 1

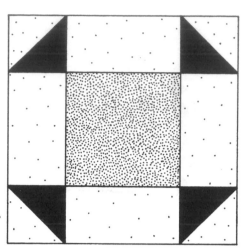

Puss in the Corner
Variation 1
   Kitty Corner, Var. 2
   Tic Tac Toe, Var. 2

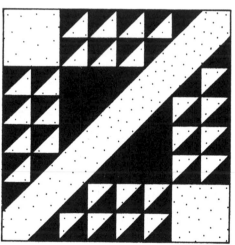

Primrose Path

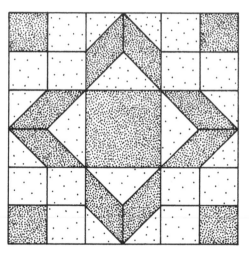

Puss in the Corner
Variation 2
   Puss in Boots

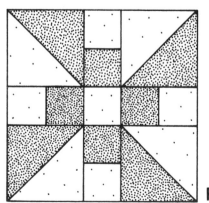

Propellor

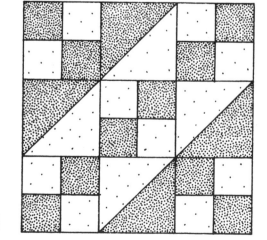

Railroad

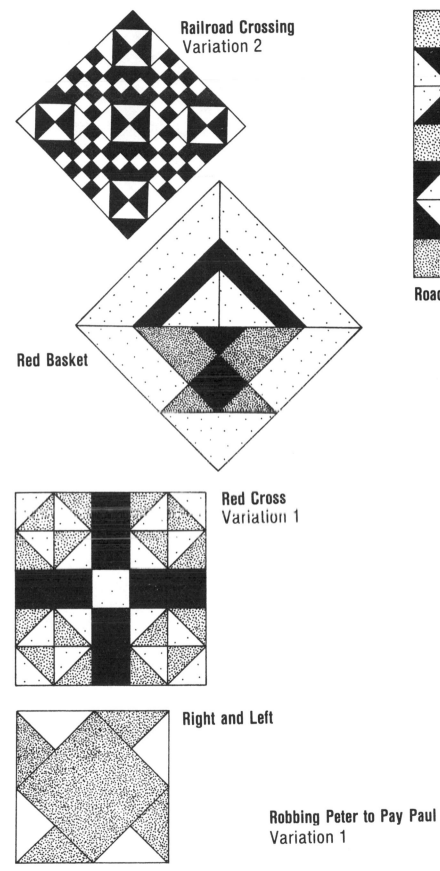

**Railroad Crossing
Variation 2**

Red Basket

**Red Cross
Variation 1**

Right and Left

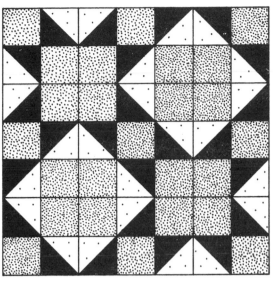

Road to California   Variation 3

Road to California   Variation 4

**Robbing Peter to Pay Paul
Variation 1**

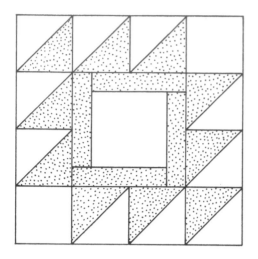

Rocky Mountain Puzzle

Sawtooth
Variation 3

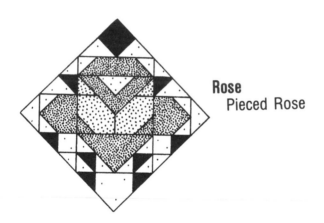

Rose
Pieced Rose

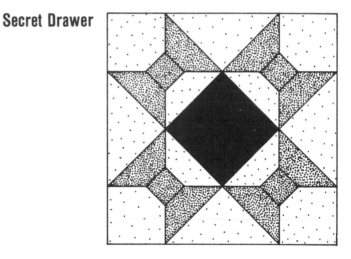

Secret Drawer

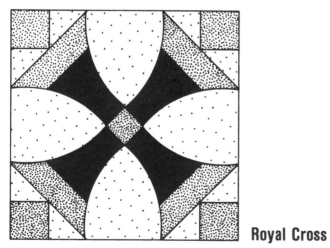

Royal Cross

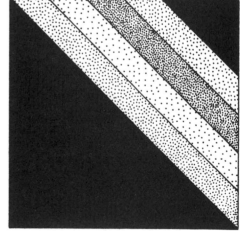

Shadows

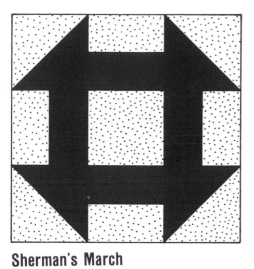

Sherman's March
Barn Door   Love Knot
Double Monkey Wrench   Monkey Wrench, Var. 2
Hole in the Barn Door   Quail's Nest
Lincoln's Platform

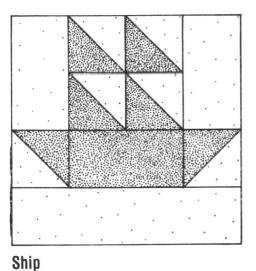

Ship

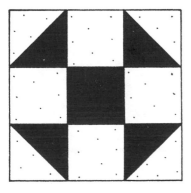

Shoofly Variation 1
Chinese Coin
Grandmother's Choice, Var. 2
Star Spangled Banner

Sister's Choice
Four-X Star
Five-Patch Star

Square and a Half

Square Within Squares

Star of Hope
Variation 1

89

Starry Lane

Swing in the Center

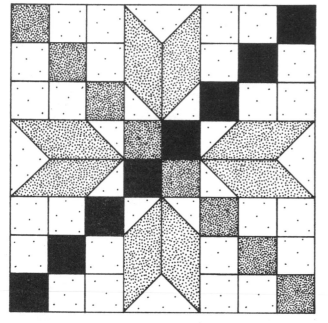

Stepping Stones
Variation 3

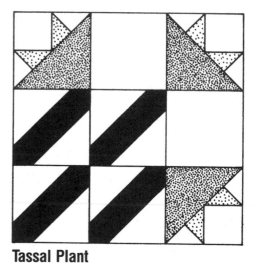

Tassal Plant

Storm at Sea   Variation 2
Rolling Stone, Var. 1

T-Blocks   Variation 2

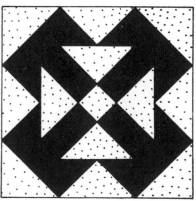

Suspension Bridge

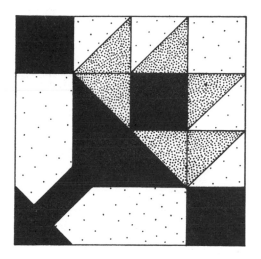

Tea Basket

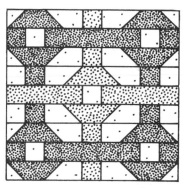

Tile Puzzle Variation 2

Thelma's Choice

Toad in the Puddle Variation 1

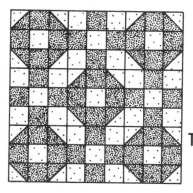

Tile Puzzle Variation 1
Improved Nine-Patch, Var. 2
Puzzled Tile

Toad in the Puddle
Variation 2
Double Square, Var. 2
Jack in the Pulpit

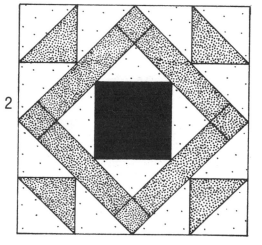

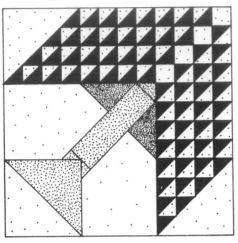

Tree of Life
Variation 1
  Pine Tree, Var. 1

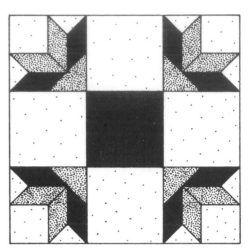

Turkey Tracks   Variation 2
Sage Bud

True Lover's Knot
Variation 1
  Rose Dream

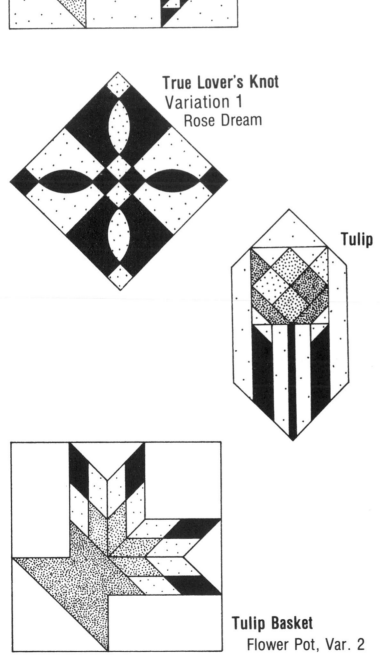

Tulip

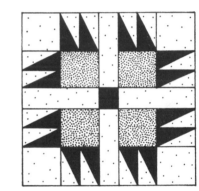

Turkey Tracks   Variation 3

Tulip Basket
  Flower Pot, Var. 2

Turnabout T

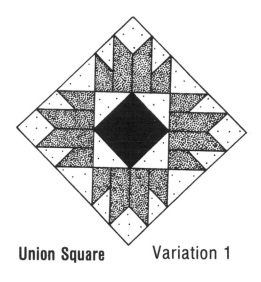

Union Square   Variation 1

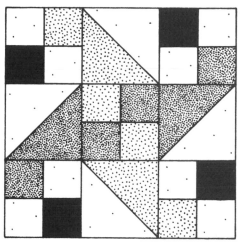

Water Wheel Variation 3

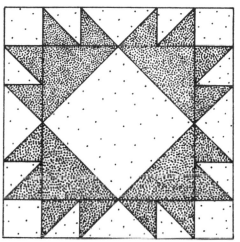

Union Square   Variation 2

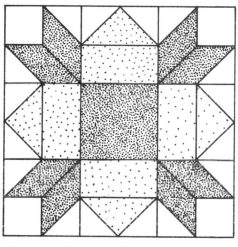

Weather Vane   Variation 2

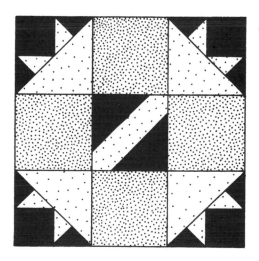

W.C.T.U.

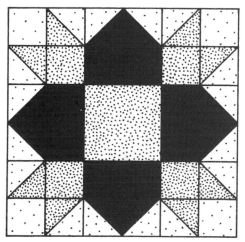

Weather Vane
Variation 3

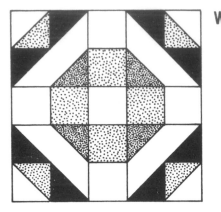

Wedding Rings

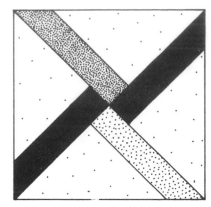

Windmill Variation 3

White Cross

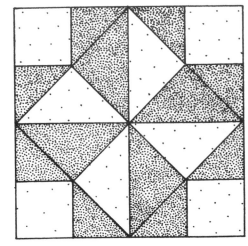

Windmill Variation 5

Wild Goose Chase Variation 3

Wishing Ring

World's Fair Variation 1

X-Quartet

X-Quisite

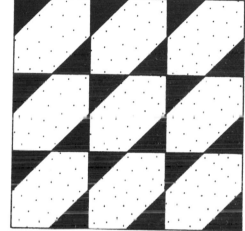

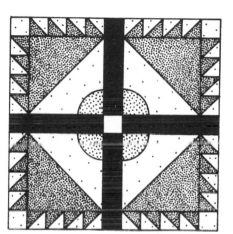

World's Fair Variation 2

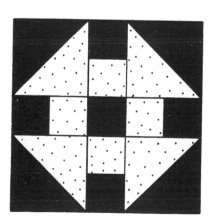

Wrench

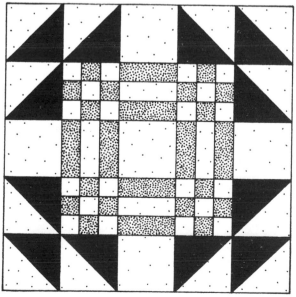

Young Man's Fancy
Goose in the Pond, Var. 2
Mrs. Wolf's Red Beauty

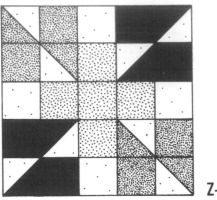

Z-Cross

Grandmother's Choice
Variation 1

SUPPLEMENT

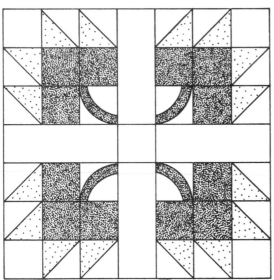

Autumn Leaf

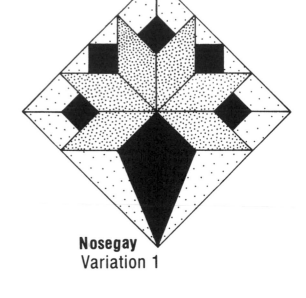

Nosegay
Variation 1

St. Gregory's Cross

54-40 or Fight

Squares

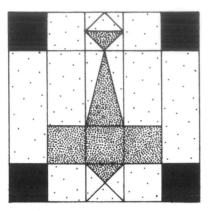

Airplane

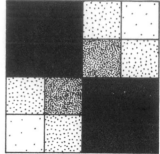

Autumn Tints
Four-Patch, Var. 3

Baby Blocks   Variation 1
  Boxes, Var. 1
  Cubework
  Heavenly Stairs
  Heavenly Steps
  Pandora's Box
  Tumbling Blocks

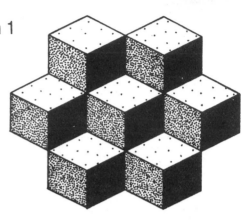

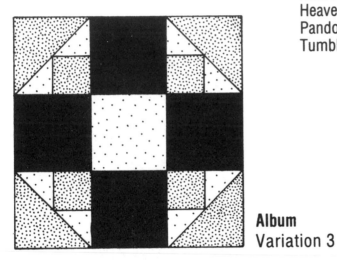

Album
Variation 3

Bachelor's Puzzle
Variation 1

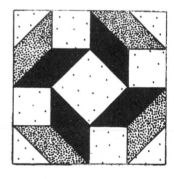

Album Patch

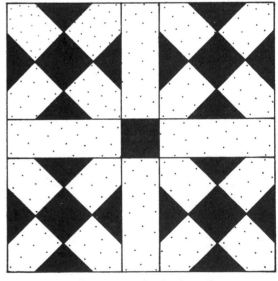

Bachelor's Puzzle   Variation 2

Basketweave

Brickwork
Bricks
Brick Wall

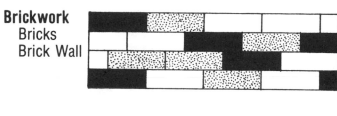

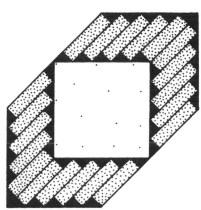

Bridal Stairway

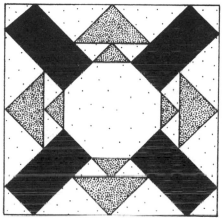

Beggar's Blocks
All Kinds

Burgoyne Surrounded
Burgoyne's Quilt
Road to California, Var. 2
Wheel of Fortune, Var. 2

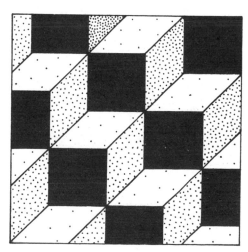

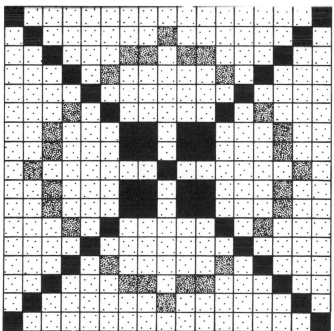

Box

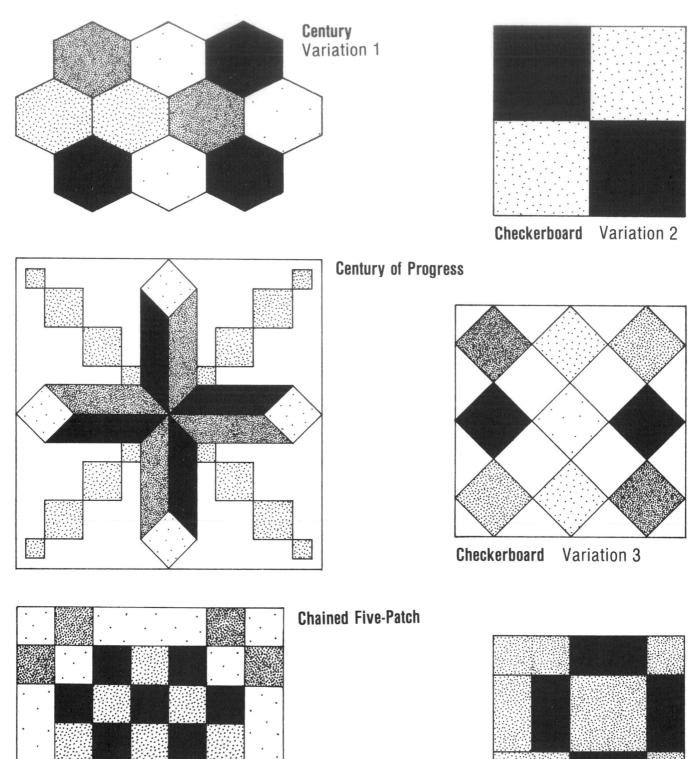

**Century
Variation 1**

Checkerboard   Variation 2

Century of Progress

Checkerboard   Variation 3

Chained Five-Patch

Children's Delight

100

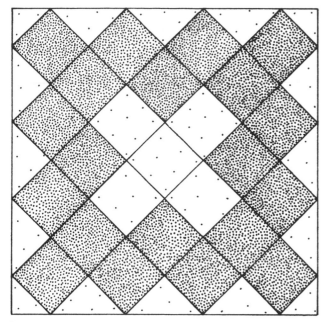

Christian Cross

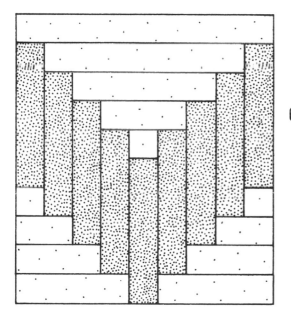

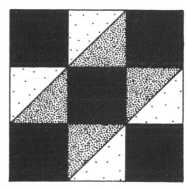

Contrary Wife

Coarsewoven
Variation 2
Finewoven, Var. 2

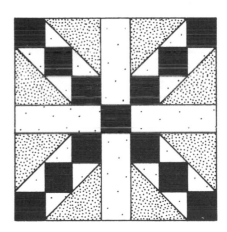

Corner Posts

Country Roads

Coffin Star
Picket Fence

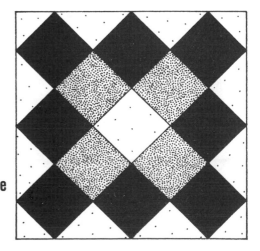

Courthouse Square

101

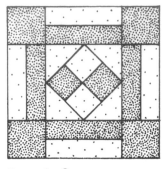

Coxey's Camp

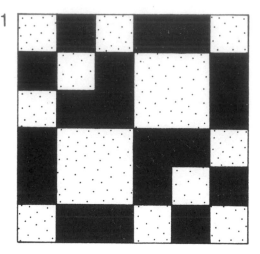

Domino Variation 1

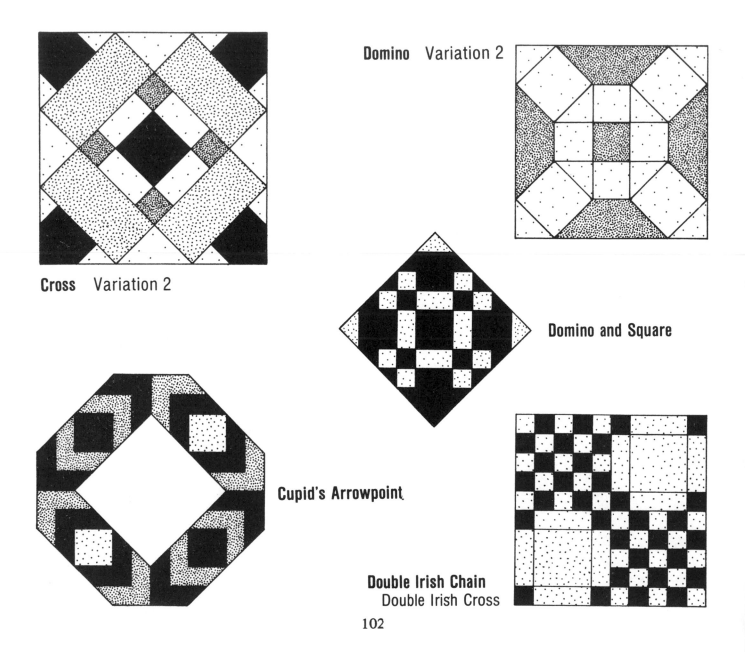

Cross Variation 2

Domino Variation 2

Domino and Square

Cupid's Arrowpoint

Double Irish Chain
Double Irish Cross

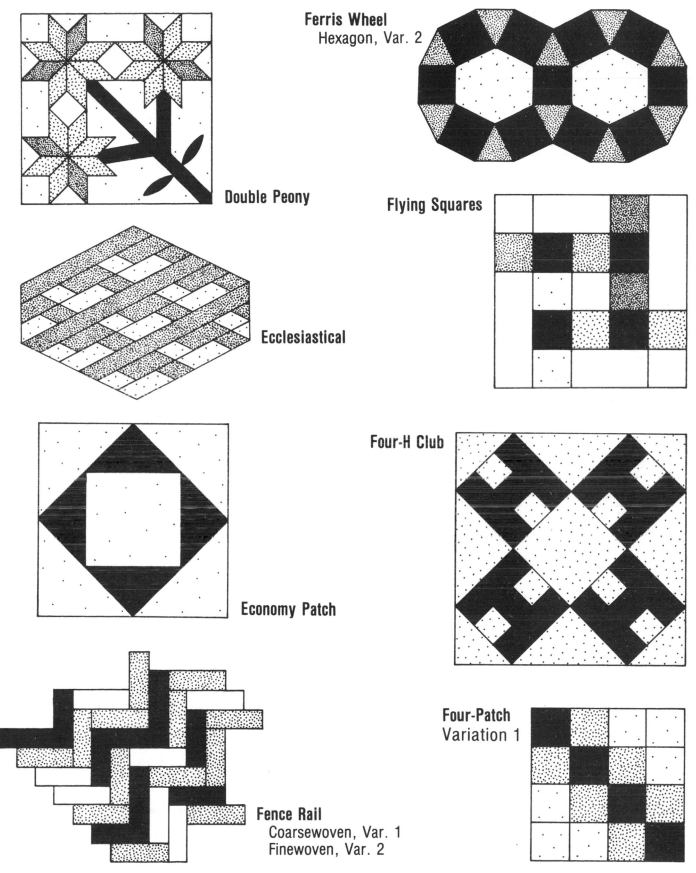

Ferris Wheel
Hexagon, Var. 2

Double Peony

Ecclesiastical

Flying Squares

Economy Patch

Four-H Club

Fence Rail
Coarsewoven, Var. 1
Finewoven, Var. 2

Four-Patch
Variation 1

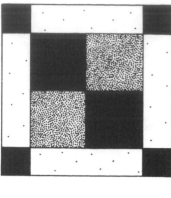

Four-Patch Variation 2

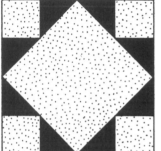

Four-Square

Friendship Square

Fundamental Nine-Patch
Single Irish Chain

Garden Maze
Sun Dial
Tangled Garter
Tirzah's Treasure

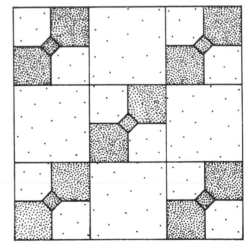

Gentleman's Bowtie
Bowtie
Joseph's Necktie

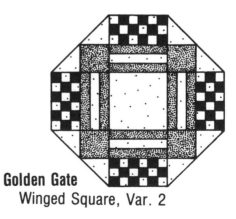

Golden Gate
Winged Square, Var. 2

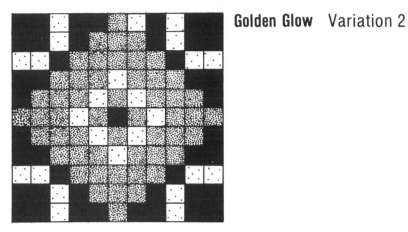

Golden Glow Variation 2

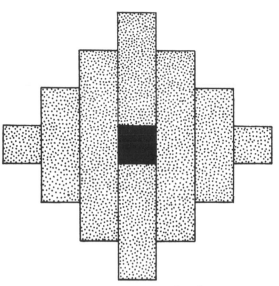

Grandma's Red and White

Granny's Flower Garden

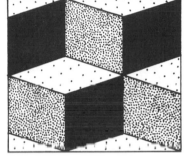

Grandmother's Flower Garden

    Flower Garden   Rainbow Tile
    French Bouquet   Rosette
    Grandma's Garden   Spider Web, Var. 1
    Honeycomb, Var. 1
    Job's Troubles, Var. 1
    Martha Washington's Flower Garden
    Mosaic

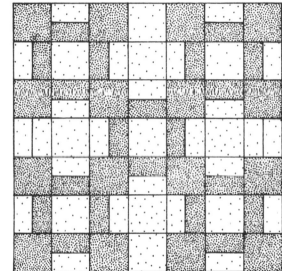

Hand

    California Oak Leaf   True Lover's Knot, Var. 2
    Sassafras Leaf

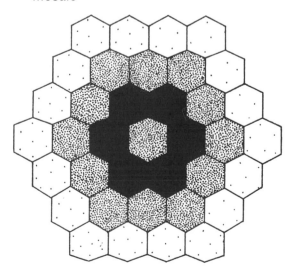

Hanging Diamond

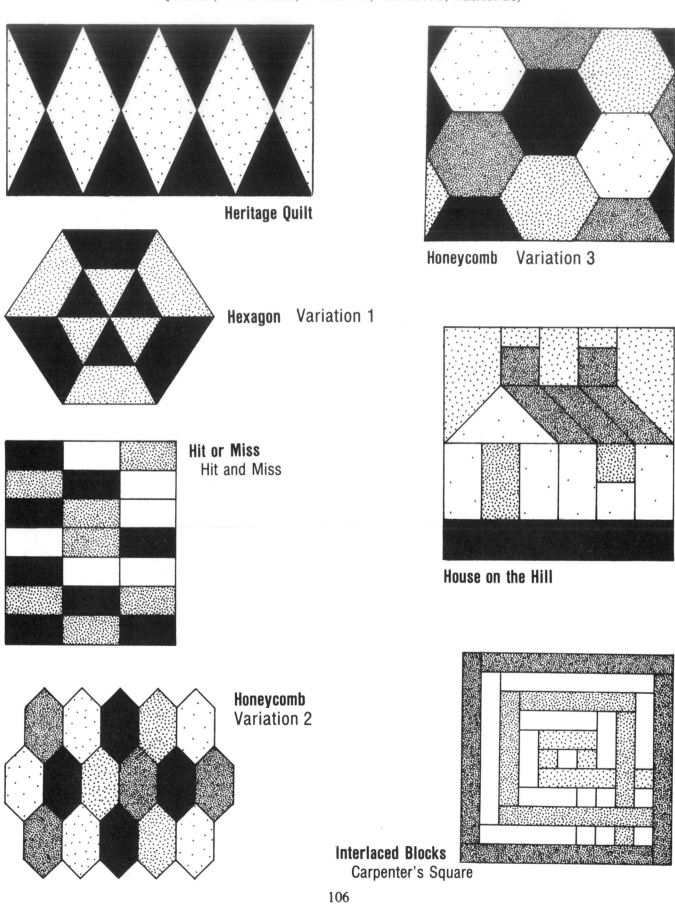

Heritage Quilt

Honeycomb   Variation 3

Hexagon   Variation 1

Hit or Miss
Hit and Miss

House on the Hill

Honeycomb
Variation 2

Interlaced Blocks
Carpenter's Square

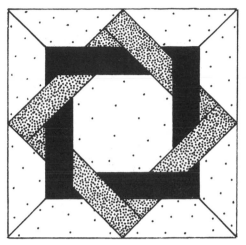

Interlocked Squares

Kansas Dugout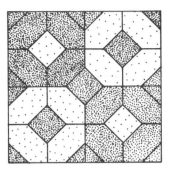

Kite's Tail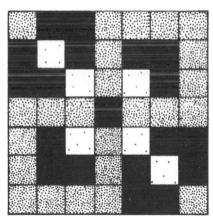

Irish Chain Variation 2
Double Nine-Patch

Leavenworth Nine-Patch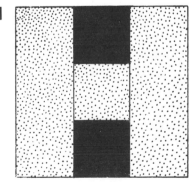

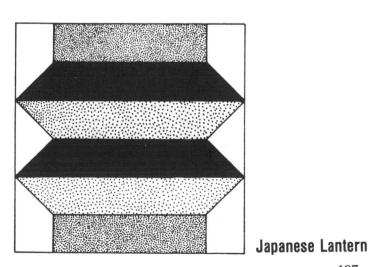

Japanese Lantern

Letter H

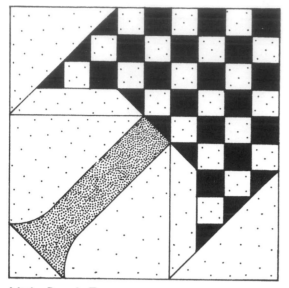

Little Beech Tree

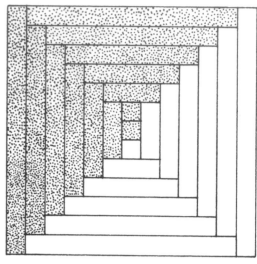

Log Cabin Variation 2
Courthouse Steps

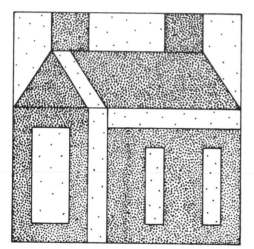

Little Red Schoolhouse

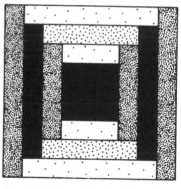

Log Cabin Variation 3

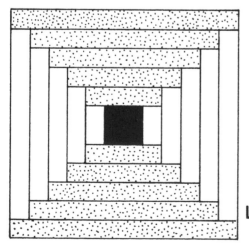

Log Cabin Variation 1
Old-Fashioned Log Cabin

Log Cabin
Variation 4

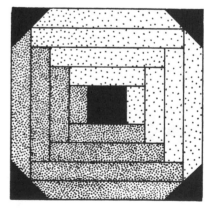

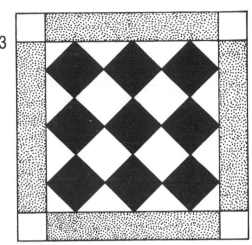

Nine-Patch Variation 3

Madam X

Nine-Patch Variation 4

Necktle Variation 1

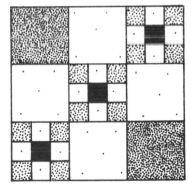

Nine-Patch Chain

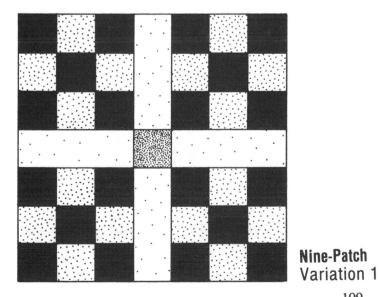

Octagon

Nine-Patch Variation 1

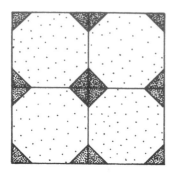

Octagons

Patience Corners

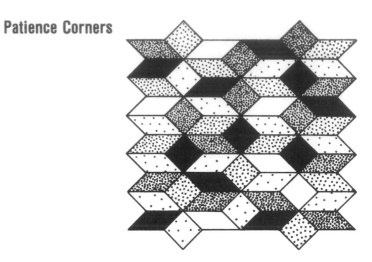

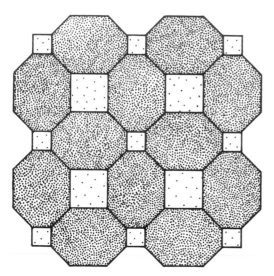

Octagon Tile

Peony

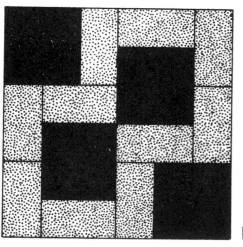

Pineapple
  Chestnut Burr
  Church Steps
  Maltese Cross, Var. 2

Patience Corner

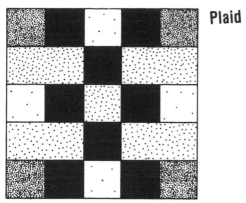

Plaid

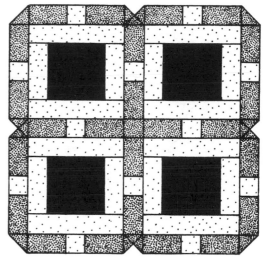

Red Cross
Variation 2

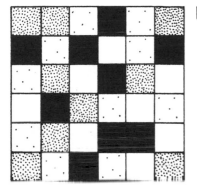

Postage Stamp

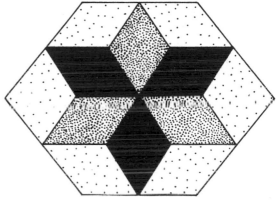

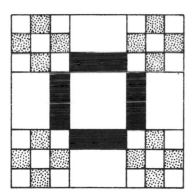

Puss in the Corner
Variation 3

Rising Star   Variation 2

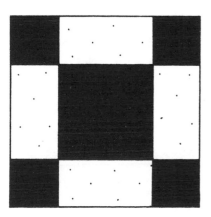

Puss in the Corner
Variation 5

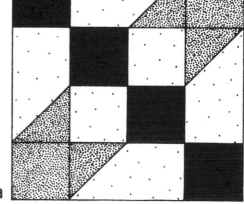

Road to Oklahoma

New Four-Patch

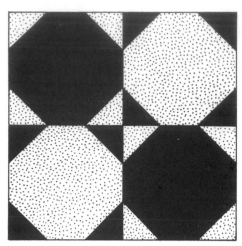

Robbing Peter to Pay Paul
Variation 5

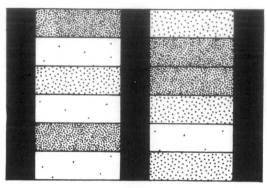

Roman Stripe   Variation 1

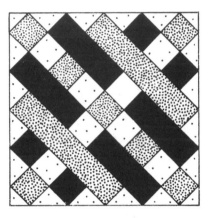

Rocky Glen
Variation 3

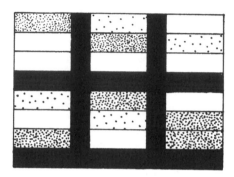

Roman Stripe   Variation 2
Roman Square, Var. 1

Roman Cross

Roman Wall

Roman Square
Variation 2
Roman Stripe Zigzag

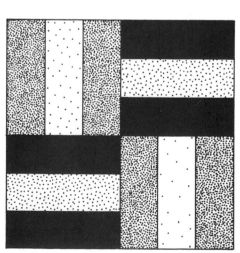

Sawtooth
Variation 7

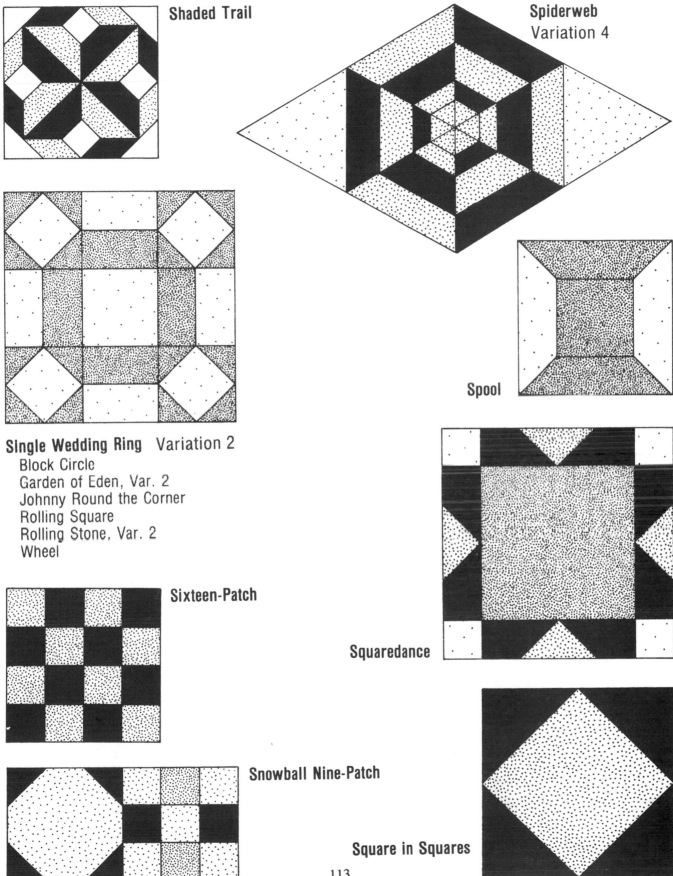

Shaded Trail

Spiderweb
Variation 4

Spool

Single Wedding Ring Variation 2
    Block Circle
    Garden of Eden, Var. 2
    Johnny Round the Corner
    Rolling Square
    Rolling Stone, Var. 2
    Wheel

Squaredance

Sixteen-Patch

Snowball Nine-Patch

Square in Squares

113

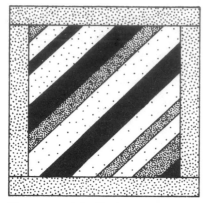

Square with Stripes

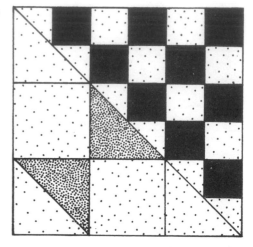

Steps to the Altar
Variation 2

Stained Glass
Church Window

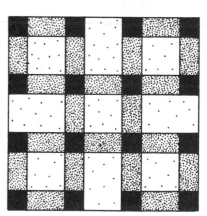

Streak O'Lightning

Strips and Squares
Strip Squares

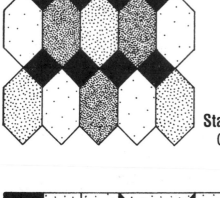

Stepping Stones
Variation 2
Arrowheads, Var. 2

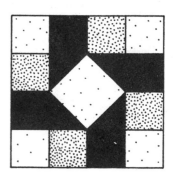

Susannah
Variation 1

Susannah
Variation 2

Susannah
Variation 3

Swastika Variation 2
Battle Ax of Thor
Catch Me if You Can

Chinese 10,000 Perfections
Favorite of the Peruvians
Heart's Seal
Mound Builders
Pure Symbol of Right Doctrine
Wind Power of the Osages

Tic Tac Toe Variation 1
Kitty Corner, Var. 1
Puss in the Corner,
Var. 4

Tile Patchwork
Chinese Puzzle,
Var. 2

Tree of Temptation

Tam's Patch

115

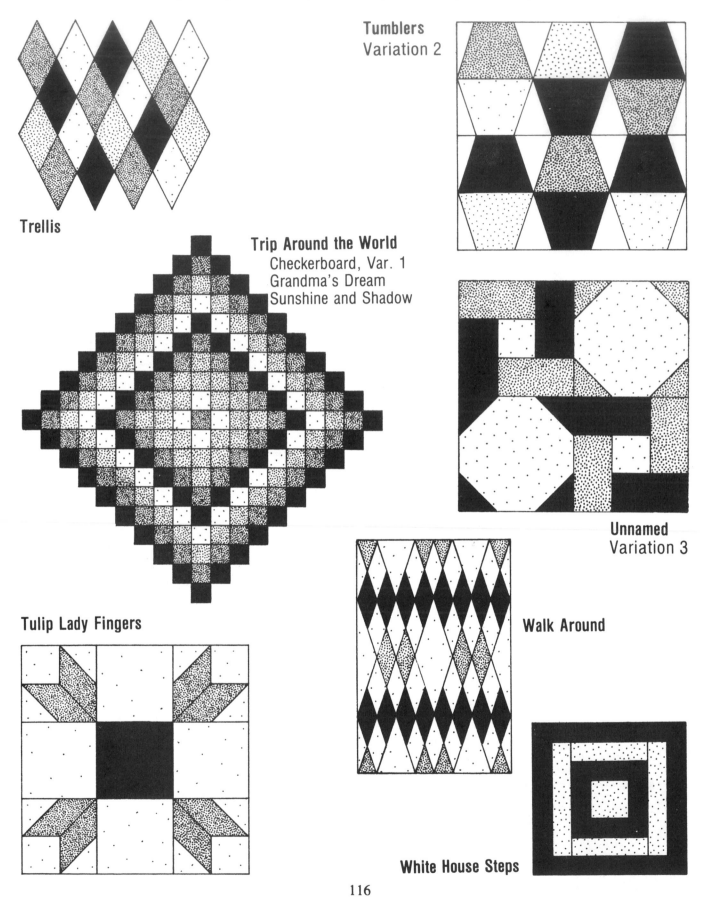

Trellis

Tumblers
Variation 2

Trip Around the World
Checkerboard, Var. 1
Grandma's Dream
Sunshine and Shadow

Unnamed
Variation 3

Tulip Lady Fingers

Walk Around

White House Steps

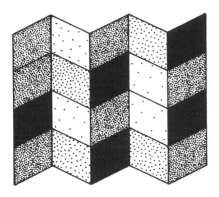

Zigzag
Variation 2
Snake Fence, Var. 2

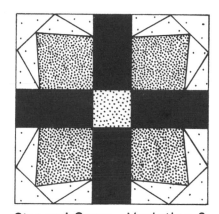

Star and Cross Variation 3

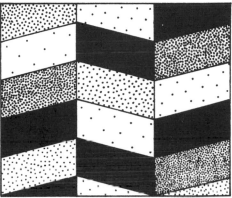

Zigzag
Variation 3

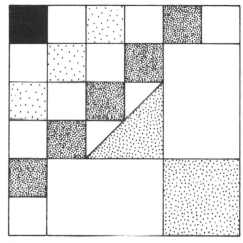

Steps to the Altar Variation 1

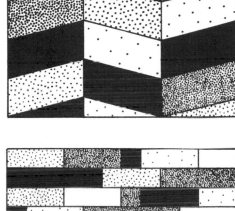

Zigzag Block

SUPPLEMENT

Flying Bats

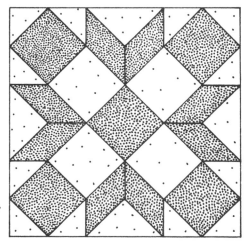

Swing in the Center
Variation 2

Appendix

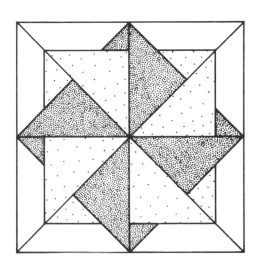

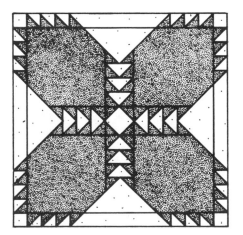

119

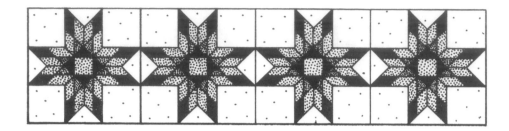

Stars

Blue Birds for Happiness

All American Star

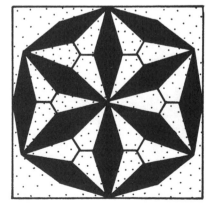

Chained Star
Variation 2

Eight Diamonds and a Star

Constellation

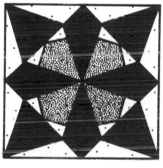

Diamond Star
Variation 3

Ella's Star

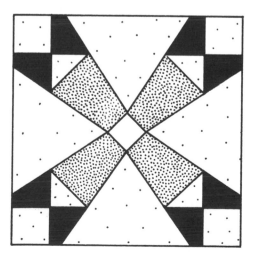

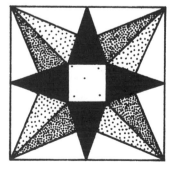

Dutch Mill
Variation 2

Exploding Star

Farmer's Wife

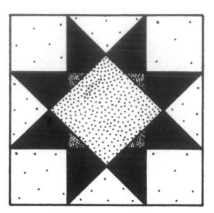

LeMoine Star
Variation 2

Guiding Star
Variation 2

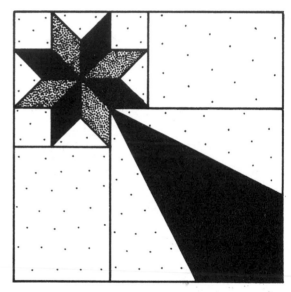

Missouri

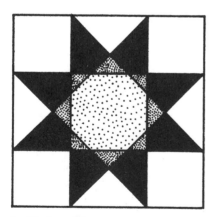

LeMoine Star
Variation 1

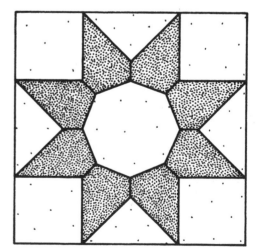

Missouri Daisy

Missouri Star   Variation 2

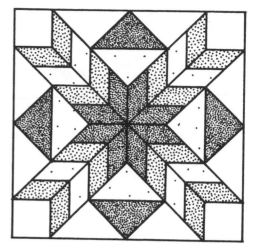

St. Elmo

Pineapple   Variation 2

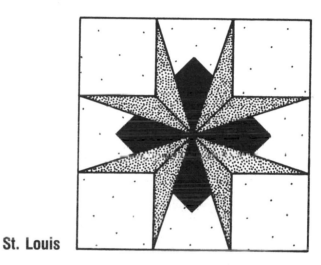

St. Louis

Rose Point

St. Louis Block

123

St. Louis Star   Variation 2

Shadow Star   Variation 2

Star
Variation 3

Shadow Star   Variation 1

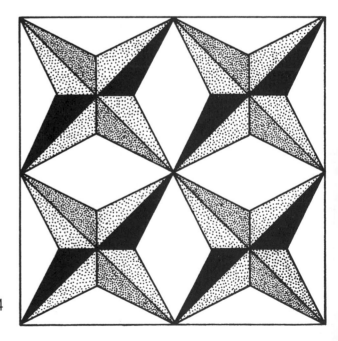

Star
Variation 4

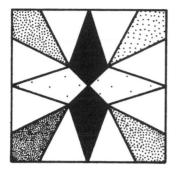

Time and Tide

Washington's Quilt

**Wandering
Diamond**

Waterlily

Triangles

Apple Tree

Christmas Tree
Variation 2

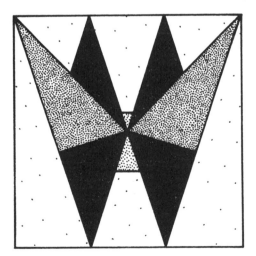

Butterflies

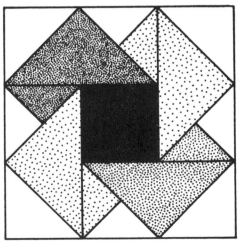

Color Wheel

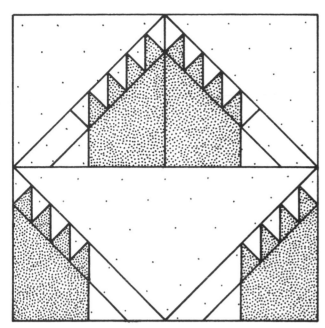

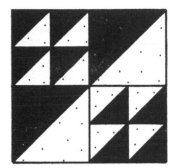

Flock of Geese
Variation 2

Delectable Mountains
Variation 4

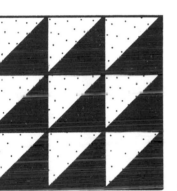

Everlasting Tree

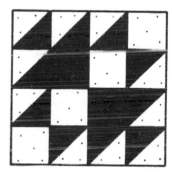

Fox and Geese
Variation 2

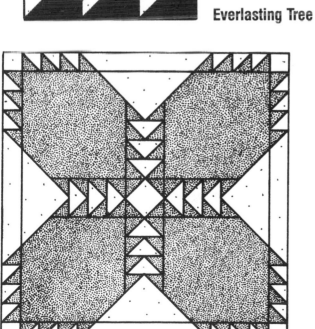

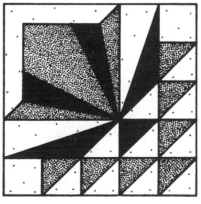

Leafy Basket

Fish in the Dish

Lighthouse

Patch as Patch Can

Lost Children

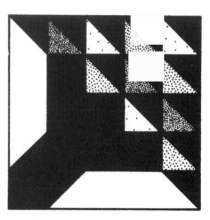

Patch Blossom

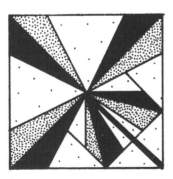

Ohio

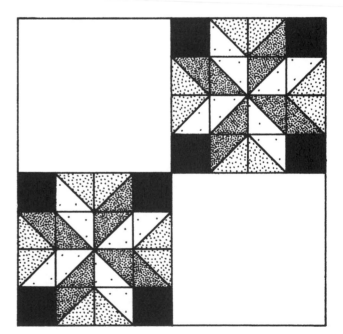

Quilter's Surprise   Variation 1

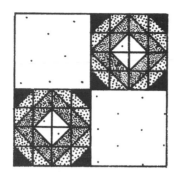

Quilter's Surprise
Variation 2

Solomon's Temple

Tree of Life
Variation 4

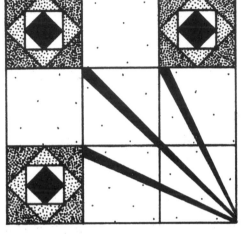

Triple Rose

Tree of Paradise   Variation 4

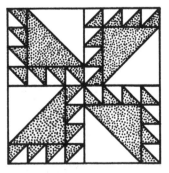

Waves of the Sea

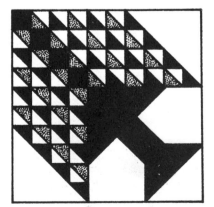

Tree of Paradise
Variation 5

Circles

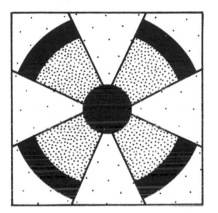

Air Ship

Boston

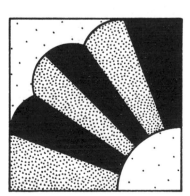

Alice

Daisy Fan

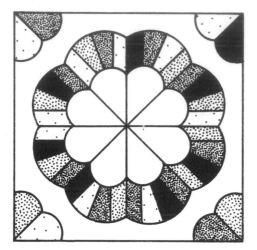

Ferris Wheel
Variation 2

Ice Cream Cone

Grandma's Red and White
Variation 2

Springtime Blossoms
Variation 2

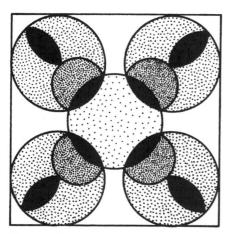

Hero's Crown

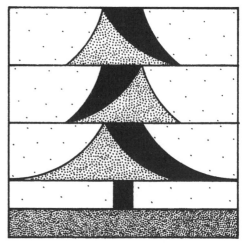

Trail of the Lonesome Pine

Combinations

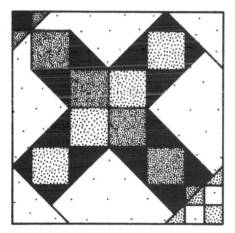

Airplane

Arkansas Traveller
Variation 2

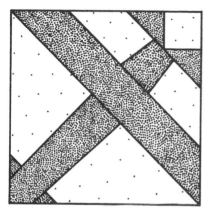

Alta-Plane

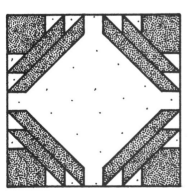

Altar Steps

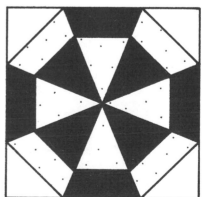

Autumn Leaves
Variation 1

Autumn Leaves
Variation 2

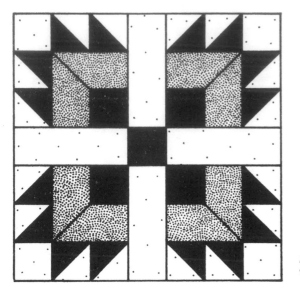

Autumn Tints
Variation 2

Basket

Bear Track
Variation 3

Buckwheat

The Breeches

Card Basket

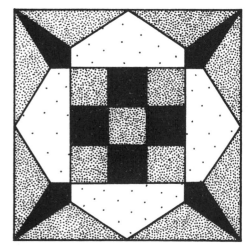

Chain of Diamonds

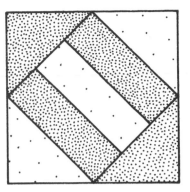

Cracker

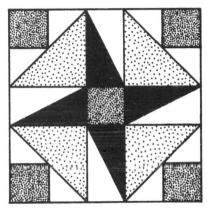

Crazy Anne

Crossroads

Cross Patch

Cross and Crown
Variation 5

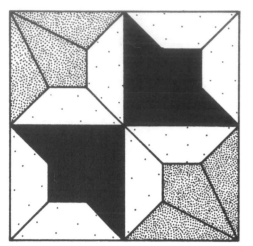

Double Tulip
Variation 2

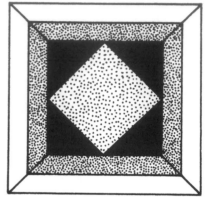

Frame a Print

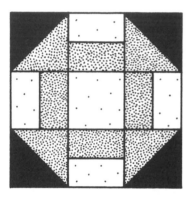

Dragon's Head

Farmer's Field

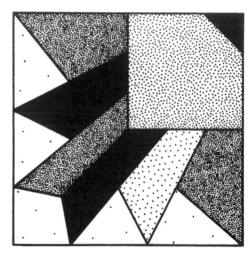

Grandmother's

Flower Basket
Variation 2

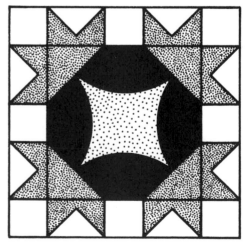

Hands All Around

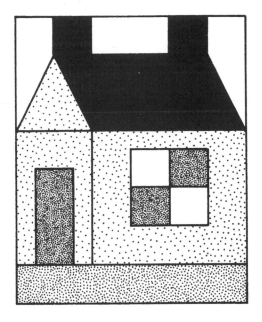

House

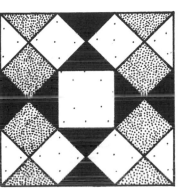

Jefferson City

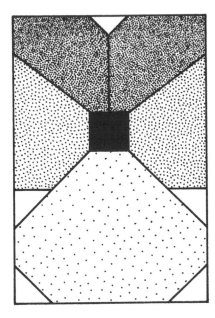

Johnny Jump-Up

Joseph's Coat
Variation 3

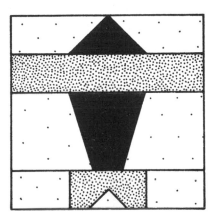

Lone Eagle

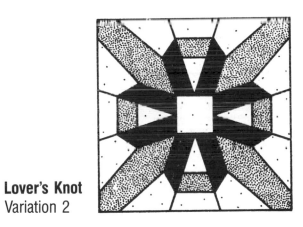

Lover's Knot
Variation 2

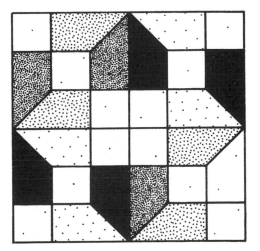

Lucky Clover

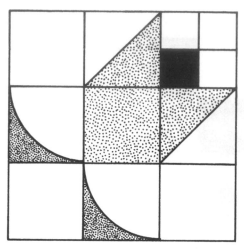

Magnolia Bud   Variation 2

**Mary Tenney Gray
Travel Club Patch**
Variation 2

Malvina's Chain

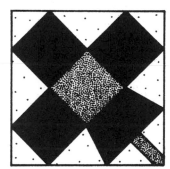

Maple Leaf
Variation 4

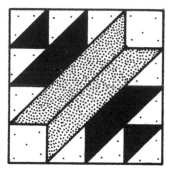

Mrs. Taft's Choice

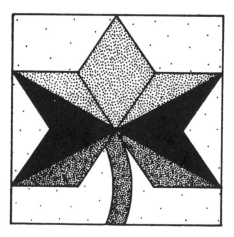

Maple Leaf
Variation 5

New Star

138

Ombre

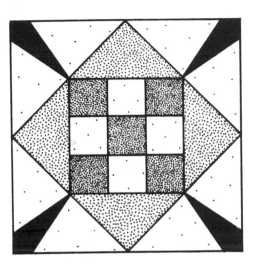

Nine-Patch Star

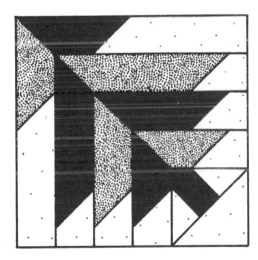

Pine Tree
Variation 5

Old Missouri

Pine Tree
Variation 6

Pinwheel
Variation 3

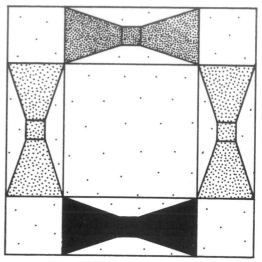

Pullman Puzzle
Variation 2

Pointed Tile

Puss in the Corner
Variation 6

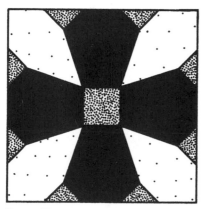

Propellor
Variation 2

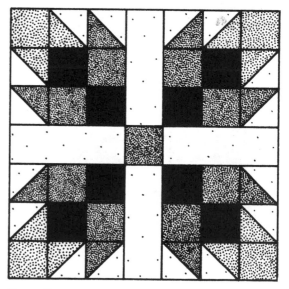

Rose Bud
Variation 2

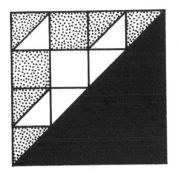

Ships at Sea

Stamp Basket

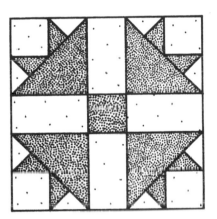

Signal

Storm at Sea
Variation 4

Spiderweb
Variation 5

Tea Leaf
Variation 3

Trees in the Park

White House Rose

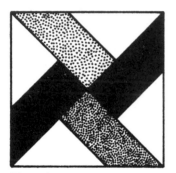

Turnabout

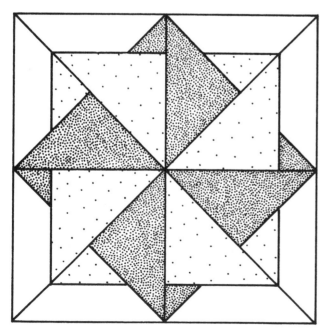

Twisting Star

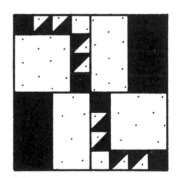

World's Fair
Variation 3

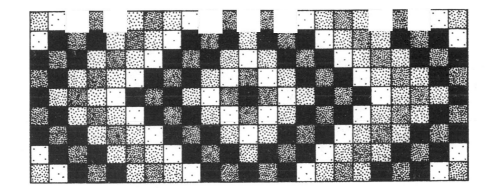

Squares

Arrow Point

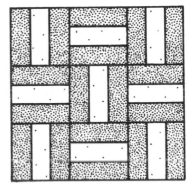

Cats and Mice
Variation 3

Aunt Sukey's Patch

Double Nine-Patch
Variation 2

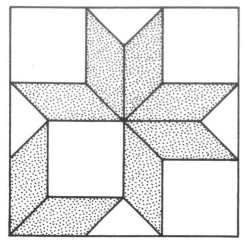

Dove at My Window

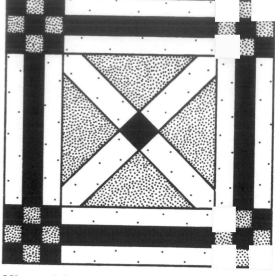

Missouri Puzzle   Variation 3

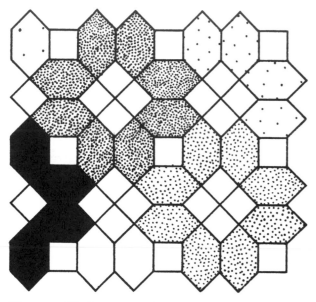

Memory Chain   Variation 2

Nine-Patch Diamond

Mexican Star   Variation 3

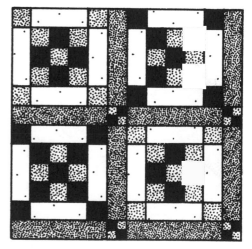

Nine-Patch Plaid

Peony Block

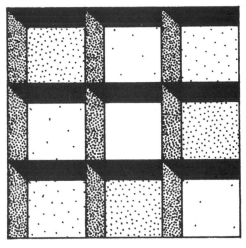

Shadow Box

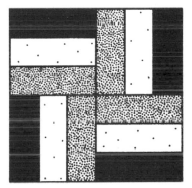

Spirit of St. Louis

Squares and Stripes

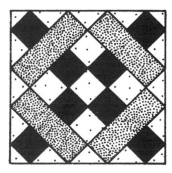

Washington Sidewalk

BIBLIOGRAPHY

Bicentennial Quilt Book, McCall's Needlework & Crafts, Editorial Director, Rosemary McMurtry, McCall Pattern Co., New York, 1975.

ERICSON, HELEN M., *Helen's Book of Basic Quiltmaking*, Groh Printing Co., Emporia, Kansas, 1973.

FINLEY, RUTH E., *Old Patchwork Quilts*, Charles T. Branford Co., Newton Centre, Mass., c. 1929, reprinted 1970.

The Foxfire Book, Editor, Eliot Wigginton, Anchor Books/Doubleday, Garden City, N.Y., 1972.

GRAFTON, CAROL BELANGER, *Traditional Patchwork Patterns*, Dover Publications, Inc., New York, 1974.

GREEN, SYLVIA, *Patchwork for Beginners*, Watson-Guptill Publications, New York, 1972.

GUTCHEON, BETH, *The Perfect Patchwork Primer*, Penguin Books Inc., Baltimore, 1973.

Heirloom Quilts, McCall's Needlework and Crafts, Editorial Director, Rosemary McMurtry, McCall Pattern Co., 1974.

HINSON, DOLORES, A., *A Quilter's Companion*, Arco Publishing, Inc., New York, 1973.

HOLSTEIN, JONATHAN, *American Pieced Quilts*, Viking Press, New York, 1972.

LARSEN, JUDITH LA BELLE & GULL, CAROL WAUGH, *The Patchwork Quilt Design & Coloring Book*, Butterick Publishing, New York, 1977.

LITHGOW, MARILYN, *Quiltmaking & Quiltmakers*, Funk & Wagnalls, New York, 1974.

MAHLER, CELINE BLANCHARD, *Once Upon a Quilt*, Van Nostrand Reinhold Co., New York, 1973.

The McCall's Book of Quilts, Editors of McCall's Needlework & Crafts Publications, Simon & Schuster/The McCall Pattern Company, New York, 1975.

McKIM, RUBY SHORT, *One Hundred and One Patchwork Patterns*, Dover Publications, Inc., New York, 1962.

Mountain Artizans, An Exhibition of Patchwork and Quilting, Museum of Art, Rhode Island School of Design, Providence, 1970.

Mrs. Danner's Fifth Quilt Book, Editor, Helen M. Ericson, Groh Printing Co., Emporia, Kansas, 1972.

Mrs. Danner's Quilts, Books 1 and 2 combined, Editor, Helen M. Ericson, Groh Printing Co., Emporia, Kansas, 1971.

Mrs. Danner's Quilts, Books 3 and 4 combined, Editor, Helen M. Ericson, Groh Printing Co., Emporia, Kansas, 1973.

ORLOFSKY, PATSY & MYRON, *Quilts in America*, McGraw-Hill Book Co., New York, 1974.

PETO, FLORENCE, *Quilts & Coverlets*, Chanticleer Press, New York, 1949.

Quilter's Newsletter Magazine, Editor-Bonnie Leman, Leman Publications, Inc., Denver.

Quilt World, Editor-Barbara Hall Pedersen.

150 Years of American Quilts, The University of Kansas Museum of Art, Lawrence, Kansas, 1973.

INDEX

INDEX TO APPENDIX